# HOLLYWOOD KNITS
# style

A Guide to
Good Knitting
and
Good Living

# HOLLYWOOD KNITS
# style

A Guide to
Good Knitting
and
Good Living

## BY SUSS COUSINS

Photographs by Deborah Jaffe

STC CRAFT | A MELANIE FALICK BOOK
A LARK PRODUCTION
STEWART, TABORI & CHANG NEW YORK

# contents

# (introduction)

IN *HOLLYWOOD KNITS,* MY FIRST BOOK, I shared my joy for knitting with thirty patterns I love to make. The pleasure of creating something out of nothing more than a few wisps of wool is so satisfying that I want to inspire as many knitters as possible to pick up their needles! Over the last few years, I've discovered that I really enjoy teaching people how to knit, whether they are well-known actresses who wander into my store in Los Angeles or readers who write in asking for help with a complicated pattern. There's something about watching a person go from tangled up in blue yarn to showing off her first scarf that makes me feel as if all is right with the world.

And when things are not so right with the world, knitting can be a comfort. The tragedy of September 11 came right in the middle of work on my first book. Since then demand for knitting classes at my store has tripled. During each session, students exchange ideas and feel such simple grace when a project is completed. These days people definitely feel the need to be together and to do something special for family and friends, both near and faraway.

I wanted to make this new book a guide to both good knitting and good living. Of course, it's filled with my latest designs, from a long fluffy scarf and funky purse to a space-dyed bikini, knitting needle cover, and an array of fun sweaters. I tried to give the collection a sense of coziness while keeping it fashion-forward. But in these pages you'll also find lots of other ways to add spice and fun to every day.

Cooking has become a focal point, for example. I've been cooking as long as I've been knitting, that is, since I was very young. So it's only natural that I serve homemade treats to the students in my classes as well as my staff, family, and friends. I count quite a few restaurateurs as pals and when we get together, we naturally wind up in the kitchen. For me, it's just as easy to cook for eight as it is to cook for two, so I'm always inviting more people to eat with us. On the pages that follow you will find some of the authentic Swedish dishes I grew up making and eating at home.

And what's life without a little music? I have a special CD mix of the perfect notes to knit by, which I hope you'll like too. Taste, sight, sound—we want to take care of all our senses while we make magic out of yarn. So touch is included as well, with some knitter's massage techniques you can practice on yourself.

Chapter 3, "Knitting Together," is my favorite section of the book. It's all about starting a knitting circle and hosting festive knitting events. Imagine a child's birthday party, a holiday party, a wedding or baby shower, or even a silent auction or school fundraiser with a knitting theme! This chapter includes guidelines for everything you need to plan the parties, from the projects and the food to the music and decor.

My store and my home inspired a section in the book on decorating with yarn (think gorgeous skeins of colorful wool arranged artfully on mantels or side tables or draped over tree branches and hung on walls). I even explain how to make your own yarn if you want to be more hands-on artsy-craftsy.

I've had quite a few readers ask for suggestions on how to turn a desire to knit into a reality. Setting aside knitting time is an ongoing challenge for most of us. In "The Knitting Life," you'll find ideas on where, when, and how to fit knitting into your schedule.

I am hoping you will use this book in every part of your home: knitting in the living room, cooking in the kitchen, even displaying it on your coffee table.

## Life since *Hollywood Knits*

The beautiful book launch party we had in my store, complete with champagne bellinis and bagels, was the beginning of what's been a whirlwind. It seems as if my book came out as knitting fever really hit in this country, so I found mentions of the book everywhere—from *In Style, Women's Wear Daily,* and *YM,* to *House & Garden* and the *Los Angeles Times.* The actress Julianne Moore, who modeled the sweater I designed for the movie *Serendipity,* tells me she was actually stopped on the street in New York, not only because she's a celebrity, but also because of the knitted poncho from my store she was wearing! Angela Bassett wrote me such a great note, congratulating me on the book and saying she would "love, love, love to come to class." She had tried knitting once in graduate school and was underwhelmed by her ability. But my book inspired her to try again. (The first time she tried to take my class, she came too late so we went to see a concert instead—being spontaneous is all part of Hollywood Knits Style!)

I appreciate just as much the hundreds of e-mails and letters I received from readers across the country. A reading teacher named Betsy told me she had just finished knitting the Little Girl Big Heart Pullover for her five-year-old neighbor, and she loved the fuzzy red yarn. She wanted to knit the hat from *How the Grinch Stole Christmas* next, so she could wear it for her young students at school.

One of my favorite letters was from a sixteen-year-old girl who lives in North Dakota, which goes to show Hollywood is a state of mind. Emily Rose had only been knitting for a year and a half when she bought my book, but she had already made four afghans, four sets of hats and mittens, a sweater, washcloths, and three baby blankets. She reported that she had knitted the Sweet Baby Cardigan and Hat in blue and white. "I couldn't resist how cute it was so I made it for my future baby. I'm not expecting, but it goes in my box for my child when I get married."

"I knit when I can't get to sleep so I can listen to the sound my needles make," wrote Emily. "I take my knitting everywhere with me. I take it to work, on trips, and just to run around town. The point is that I just love to knit and it's very hard for me to put it down." A girl after my own heart!

RIGHT: *A typical gathering of our Knitting Group, or what I call the soul of Suss Design.*

In fact, working on the book brought me back in a wonderful way to handknitting, which I hadn't been as involved with since launching my line of machine-knit designs for department stores. I've been twisting my own yarn lately and experimenting with hand-dyeing. An English woman, whom I got to know when we worked together on dyeing the sweaters I made for *Scooby Too,* inspired me. I took some plain clean cotton yarn and stayed up until three in the morning dipping it into different colors. I created a sort of tie-dyed look for my own new yarn line. The appeal of that yarn led to a lot of the fresh patterns that follow.

Another source of creative inspiration has been my digital camera. I find I can't leave home without it anymore. I'm constantly stopping the car to take a snapshot of something interesting that I can incorporate into a project or into the layout of the store.

I've included some patterns that first appeared in films, videos, and television shows. I think you'll find a good mix, from the legwarmers Jennifer Lopez danced in on her *Flashdance* MTV special to the hats and sweaters I made for Russell Crowe and other actors in *Master and Commander.*

Doing custom work for film made me think: Why not share designing skills with my customers? So now at Suss Design customers can take a beginning knitting or crochet class to learn the basics and can then move on to Make Your Own Hat, My First Sweater, Poncho Class, Fantasy Throw Class, or Baby Set Class. A really popular offering is our Knitting Group, where people get help on whatever they're working on and meet other knitters. It's like the soul of Suss Design.

As I wrote in my last book, I know you may not be able to take my classes. But this time around I can share with you my *livsgladje,* or joie de vivre, whether it's on the subject of knitting, food, home décor, parties, friends, music, or mothering. Because I do think life is all wrapped up like one big ball of luscious yarn, *Hollywood Knits Style*!

**(CHAPTER 1)**

# why not knit?

ONE OF THE OLDEST PASTIMES IN THE WORLD, knitting is also one of the most popular crafts today, as you no doubt know if you're reading this book! From boardrooms to chat rooms, knitters are everywhere. Smart college students have formed knitting groups with clever names like the Knit Wits. At one large bookstore chain, a weekly Knitters Gathering is well attended. Men—lots of them!—and women, young and old, knit on subways, at meetings, on vacation. And why not? To start with nothing more than a simple ball of yarn and end up, many relaxing hours later, with a sweater, a pair of socks, or even a bikini—I think that's exciting.

Each time I hear the click of the needles, I can't help but think for a moment about all those knitters who came before me. The yarn is like a link to a million other knitters over the last thousand years. I imagine myself as a peasant making a rough shawl to wear in the fields, or a hosier knitting a stocking for a queen, or a young girl making a warm sweater for her brother fighting as a soldier in the Great War. Knitting draws you into a continuum of people, places, and time as history unwinds with the yarn.

## The Origins of Wool circa 4000 B.C.

Woolen fabric is made from the fleece of sheep and was probably the first animal fiber to be made into cloth. Methods of spinning wool into yarn developed about 4000 B.C., most likely in the region of the Mediterranean Sea. By 50 A.D., England had its first wool factory, built in Winchester by the Romans. Today, different breeds of sheep produce about two hundred types of wool around the world.

The actual origins of knitting have never been completely revealed. We know it's been practiced in different parts of the globe for centuries, and that it most likely began about 200 A.D. in Arabia or Persia. As Middle Eastern trade began expanding to Europe, Europeans were introduced to knitting during the 600s. By the Middle Ages, there were knitting guilds, like workers' unions, and knitting became an industry like weaving. Knitters had to serve as apprentices for six years before they could enter the guild! Lucky for my students I don't make them apprentice that long.

A history of knitting has even been traced in the most unexpected locations among the most unexpected classes of people. In 1854, when Japan signed the "Agreements for Friendly Relations between the U.S. and Japan," Americans were given access to the country and a wave of Western influence took hold. Japanese government and its military were restructured according to Western models. Samurai found both their influence and income waning, and to supplement their earnings, some of them took to knitting the gloves and socks that were among the new standard items of military apparel. In particular, they would knit *Tabi,* a Japanese sock whose split toes provided the extra freedom of movement required by warriors. You might think that knitting is exactly opposite to the kind of activity a Samurai would be trained to do; it just goes to show that anyone can learn to knit!

## Knitting in Scandinavia and with Uncle Sam

It makes sense, when you think about it, that knitting has always been most popular in the coldest climates, where creating warm clothing is a matter of survival. Think of the fishermen's sweaters of Ireland, the Peruvian mountain hats, and of course those colorful scarves and mittens in my own Sweden.

In Sweden knitting is common in every household. It's an ancient tradition, but we also think of it as part of everyday life. When I was growing up, my mother and grandmother were always working on various knitting projects. I loved to knit with them, and I definitely had a head start on my classmates. Although all Swedish boys and girls are taught to knit, crochet, and sew when they are about seven years old, I think I was regarded as unusual because I started when I was even younger, around four or five, and enjoyed it much more than my friends. A lot of men in Sweden knit, and no one thinks twice about it. This may be because it's fairly common in Sweden for men to stay home and take care of their children while women go to work.

The attitude toward knitting is different in the United States. Although knitting is now popular here, there are still large numbers of people who have never tried it or even seen a knitting needle. Many of my students have barely had any exposure to it when they start taking my classes. That's why in writing this book I've tried to make everything as simple and clear as possible, all the while communicating the spirit of the knitting tradition with which I grew up.

## Getting Started

I hope by now you can't wait to start knitting. The first piece of advice I always give people who say they want to learn is to find a good teacher. If you happen to live in Los Angeles, sign up for one of my beginner classes, and I guarantee you'll learn how to cast on, knit, purl, bind off, increase, decrease, and understand gauge—all you need to know—in three weeks! Otherwise, call or visit your local yarn shop for recommendations on classes or private teachers. If you're lucky enough to have a friend or relative

who knits, you can make a deal to trade a few knitting lessons for something they need: babysitting, computer tutoring, a home-cooked meal. Be creative!

As I explained in my first book, besides yarn and needles, there isn't much else you absolutely must have to start knitting. So have fun picking out some of the following items:

**KNITTING NEEDLES:** In a few basic materials and sizes, such as bamboo, aluminum, or casein, sizes 7 though 19.

**SCISSORS:** Small and sharp are the best. I like Fiskars brand but try them on your hands for a comfortable "fit" before investing.

**TAPE MEASURE:** For knitting, always use a tape measure made out of cloth, wood, or plastic rather than metal, which can snag the wool.

**STITCH GAUGE:** A necessary object if accuracy in the pattern is important.

**CROCHET HOOK:** Although you are a knitter now, you will use crochet for finishing pieces. A collection of hooks in sizes A through S comes in handy.

**POINT PROTECTORS:** These help keep the yarn from slipping off the pointed end of the needle so you don't lose any stitches. They also prevent the needles from poking through your knitting bag—or your cat from unraveling your work.

**TAPESTRY NEEDLES:** These large needles with big eyes are important for sewing pieces of knitting together using yarn.

## about scissors

I always have a collection of scissors on hand: big, small, pointed, and even clumsy, heavy-duty ones. Fiskars is the brand I grew up with, so I tend to buy those most often. But I don't really care all that much about the brand; what's most important is that it's a quality scissor that fits my hand well. For knitting purposes, small and pointy scissors are very useful for cutting yarn. I also use them to unstitch a seam. You will need compact scissors to take with you at all times. In my store I sell a small pair that folds up so the point won't poke you when you are rummaging through your bag for them. Different kinds of fabrics and yarns need different kinds of scissors, but they should always be very sharp, or they might ruin the material. Although I make sure to keep most of my scissors sharpened, I usually don't sharpen my smallest scissors because it's too difficult. Instead I replace them when they get dull. Still, there are some scissors that I will always treasure. I love one engraved pair I found at a flea market and always keep them handy.

## 9 sample swatch ideas

Even though making a gauge swatch is one of the most important steps to success in knitting, a lot of knitters don't like to do it—they just want to start their project right away. The problem is that if you don't match the gauge (the number of stitches and rows per inch) called for in the pattern, your project is likely to turn out misshapen. Here are a few fun uses for swatches. For some you'll need to sew a collection of swatches together.

- Coffee or tea cup cozy
- Coaster (with crocheted edging on all four sides)
- Doll/stuffed animal blankie
- Book or journal cover
- Knitting bag
- Pillow cover
- Scarf or hat
- Invitation envelope (fold swatch in half and sew up sides)
- Wraparound skirt

## choosing projects

To help you select projects to knit from this book, I've rated each one, from Cinchy for Starters (easy, suitable for beginners) to Step up and Knit (the next step up, a bit more time, perhaps requires shaping or other finishing) and finally Hot Knitters (for advanced beginners and beyond).

## memory scarf

Remember all the projects you've knitted over the years by making a scarf out of the leftover yarn. Don't think about a pattern, feel free to knit with different textures and stitch patterns—just cast on and be creative. For fun, try knitting with two or more thin yarns together. Or run a novelty yarn like a metallic alongside a more subdued traditional yarn. Whatever you do, the result will be unpredictable and full of knitting memories.

(A KNIT AFFAIR)

# mother-daughter
## knitting group

### Occasion/Theme
Spend quality time with your daughter, along with a few of her close friends and their mothers. You'll learn about each other and yourselves. Start the knitting group when your daughter is about seven years old, and chances are you'll share the joy of knitting together for many years to come.

### Time/Season
Unwind and knit during a Saturday morning brunch to slow down the pace of the back-to-school season.

### Project
Knitting Needle Cover

### Music
Alternate mother-daughter favorites.

### Variations
Try the Suss Knit Kit scarf for your project (see page 134 to order). It is offered in 12 colors and includes instructions for different fringe treatments, so it can work for both mothers and daughters, conservative or funky.

## menu

**Ginger Beer**

**Chicken Satay with Spicy Peanut Sauce**

**Grandma's Cornbread**

**Swedish Apple Cake with Vanilla Sauce**

(all recipes on page 136)

# flashy
## leg warmers

THE MUST-HAVE LEG WARMERS—because Jennifer Lopez danced away in them in the *Flashdance* MTV special. I made them in black for MTV and burgundy with gold Lurex for *Shall We Dance,* her movie with Richard Gere. This pattern, which is longer and thicker than Jennifer's and has a ribbed top, is a tiny bit toned down, but it still sparkles. Wear over boots and jeans for a shopping spree or with heels and a dress for evening.

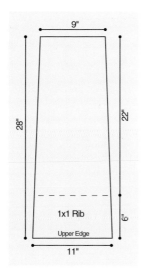

**Experience Level:** Cinchy for Starters

**Size:** One size fits most

**Finished Measurements:** 28" long x 5$\frac{1}{2}$" wide (thigh/top edge); 4$\frac{1}{2}$" wide (ankle/lower edge)

**Materials:** 4 skeins Classic Elite Lush (50% angora/50% wool; 1.75 ounces/ 50 grams; 124 yards/114 meters), color #4434 burgundy

LEFT: *You don't have to be a dancer to love these leg warmers.*

4 skeins London Yarns Sinflex Lurex (60% cupro/40% metallicized fibers; 8 ounces/20 grams; 162 yards/150 meters), color #111 pink

1 pair size 9 (5.5mm) needles, or size to obtain gauge

1 pair size 8 (5mm) needles, or size to obtain gauge

Tapestry needle

### Gauge:

20 stitches and 24 rows = 4"/10 cm in Stockinette stitch using larger needles and 1 strand of each yarn held together

24 stitches and 28 rows = 4"/10 cm in 1x1 Rib using smaller needles and 1 strand of each yarn held together

**How to Knit:** Using smaller needles and 1 strand of each yarn held together, beginning at upper edge, cast on 54 stitches.

Work in 1x1 Rib as follows:

Row 1: *Knit 1, purl 1; repeat from *across.

Row 2: Knit the knit stitches and purl the purl stitches as they face you.

Repeat Rows 1 and 2 for 1x1 Rib; WHILE AT THE SAME TIME,

Shape leg: Decrease 1 stitch on each side every 10 rows for a total of 2 times, then work even in 1x1 Rib until piece measures 6" from the beginning, ending after a wrong side row.

Change to larger needles and Stockinette stitch (knit one right side row and purl one wrong side row), WHILE AT THE SAME TIME, continue shaping leg.

Decrease 1 stitch on each side every 20 rows for a total of 5 times—40 stitches remaining. Work even until piece measures 28" from the beginning.

Bind off the remaining stitches.

Make a second Leg Warmer the same as the first.

**Finishing:** Fold one Leg warmer in half lengthwise, with right sides facing each other. Using the tapestry needle, threaded with 1 strand of each yarn held together, sew edges together.

Repeat for the other Leg warmer.

# long
## men's scarf

THIS SCARF IS BASED ON THE CARDIGAN I did for the *Starsky & Hutch* movie with Ben Stiller. The cardigan was quite complicated, so I've introduced a scarf instead in the same yarn and colors. Worked in Seed stitch, it's great for the special guy in your life, especially if he lets you borrow it once in awhile.

**Experience Level:** Cinchy for Starters

**Size:** One size fits all

**Finished Measurements:**

75" long x 8" wide (without fringe)

**Materials:**

4 skeins Suss Ull (100% wool; 2 ounces/57 grams; 215 yards/198 meters), color aran

1 skein Suss Ull (100% wool; 2 ounces/57 grams; 215 yards/198 meters), color ash

1 skein Suss Ull (100% wool; 2 ounces/57 grams; 215 yards/198 meters), color storm

1 pair size 11 (8mm) needles, or size to obtain gauge

1 size G/6 (4mm) crochet hook

**Gauge:**

12 stitches and 16 rows = 4"/10 cm in Seed stitch, using a double strand of yarn

Note: Aran may be carried up the edge of piece when not in use, to eliminate extra ends to weave in. Cut and rejoin other colors as needed.

**How to Knit:**

Using a double strand of aran, cast on 22 stitches.

Work in Seed stitch for the entire length of the scarf, as follows:

Row 1: *Knit 1, purl 1; repeat from *across.

Row 2: *Purl 1, knit 1; repeat from *across. (Note: Knit the purl stitches and purl the knit stitches as they face you.)

Repeat Rows 1 and 2.

Work a total of 10 rows using aran.

LEFT: *Longtime friend Ulf Andersson, a Swedish clothing designer, wears a scarf inspired by the movie* Starsky & Hutch.

Join a double strand of storm; work 6 rows.

Join a double strand of ash; using aran and ash, continuing in Seed stitch, begin as follows:

*Knit 1 with aran, purl 1 with ash; repeat from *across. Work 12 rows, alternating colors as established.

Join a double strand of storm; work 6 rows.

Using the double strand of aran; work 232 rows.

Join a double strand of storm; work 6 rows.

Join a double strand of ash; work 12 rows as above, alternating aran and ash.

Join a double strand of storm; work 6 rows.

Using the double strand of aran, work 10 rows; bind off all stitches in pattern–a total of 300 rows; the piece measures approximately 75" in length.

### Finishing:

Weave in ends.

Using the crochet hook and a double strand of aran, single crochet around outer edges. (Note: Work 3 stitches into the same stitch in each corner to round off nicely.)

Fringe:

Cut 32 strands of aran, 32 strands of ash, and 32 strands of storm, each 20" in length.

Combine 2 strands of each color (16 groups of 6 strands total).

Fold each group in half; using the crochet hook, pull one group through the end of the scarf, form a loop and pull ends through the loop. Attach 8 fringes each to the top and bottom edges, spacing them 1" apart.

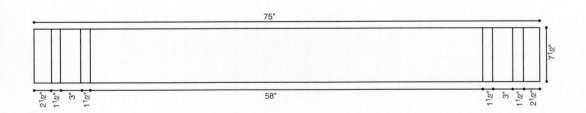

# knitting
## needle cover

I MADE THIS STYLISH NEEDLE HOLDER in fabric for my store and then realized it could be fun to knit it in your own color combos. I suggest one combination, but feel free to go wild. The yarn is a soft, four-ply cotton. This holder can comfortably hold five pairs of needles and five crochet hooks, enough for a variety of projects. It's sure to keep you neat and organized.

**Experience Level:** Cinchy for Starters

**Finished Measurements:** 21" long x 20 1/2" wide

**Materials:**

2 skeins Suss Bomull (100% cotton; 4 ounces/114 grams; 190 yards/175 meters), color camel

1 skein Suss Bomull (100% cotton; 4 ounces/114 grams; 190 yards/175 meters), color grape

1 pair size 9 (5.5mm) needles, or size to obtain gauge

1 size G/6 (4mm) crochet hook

Tapestry needle

**Gauge:**

16 stitches and 20 rows = 4"/10 cm

**How to Knit:**

Cover: Using grape yarn, cast on 84 stitches.

Work in Stockinette stitch (knit one right side row and purl one wrong side row) for a total of 24 rows—piece measures approximately 5" from the beginning, ending after a wrong side row.

Change to camel yarn and work in Stockinette stitch until piece measures 30" from the beginning, ending after a right side row.

Shape edge: Bind off 14 stitches every other row 6 times—length along right-hand edge will be approximately 32".

Using the crochet hook and grape yarn, work 1 row of single crochet along the bound-off edge.

**Finishing:**

Place knitted panel flat in front of you with the wrong side facing you and the 5" grape edge facing away from you. Fold the shaped camel edge up toward center of piece—9" on the longer side, 7" on the shorter side (see diagram). Pin sides in

place. Using the crochet hook, single crochet one side together, beginning at the lower edge. Without cutting the yarn, single crochet around the flap and down the other side, joining the remaining side seam and ending at the lower edge. (Note: Work 3 stitches into the same stitch in each corner to round off nicely.)

Needle pockets: Beginning at 9" side, place markers along lower edge as follows: Mark 3 pockets, 2" in width; 6 pockets, 1 1/2" in width; and 5 pockets, 1" in width (see diagram).

Using the tapestry needle and grape yarn, sew lines in back stitch at each marker, from the lower edge to the shaped edge as follows: Draw the needle up. In one motion, insert the needle a little behind where the yarn emerged and draw it up the same distance in front. Continue from right to left, by inserting the needle where the yarn first emerged.

Insert needles. Fold flap (5" grape edge) down to cover top of needles and prevent them from falling out.

Tie: Using the crochet hook and grape yarn, chain stitch a tie approximately 50" long.

Fold the Needle Cover 3 times lengthwise, by folding each side toward the center. Tie the crocheted chain around the Needle Cover. (Note: If desired, the crocheted chain tie may be attached to the center back.)

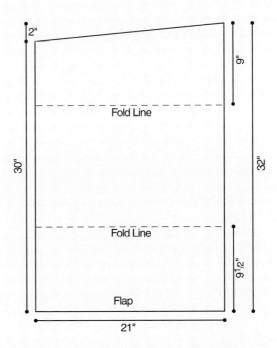

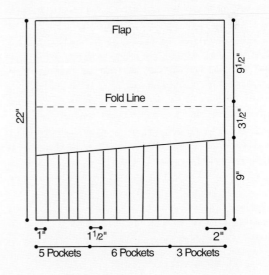

LEFT: *A knitting needle cover makes a thoughtful gift for members of your knitting group.*

# the ultimate
# two-way poncho

**ONE DAY WHEN KATEY SEGAL** came into the store to find a project to knit, I was wearing my solid black version of this poncho. Katey loved it and immediately decided to make one in these soft muted stripes and one in black also. Striped or solid, it's easy to knit—only one piece! Ponchos are so comfortable, especially this two-way design, because you can wear it off the shoulder or with a V-neck in front, and it can look either elegant or casual. I love it with my jeans and boots.

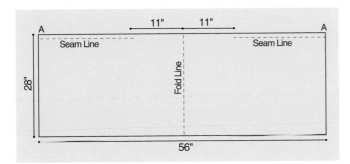

**Experience Level:** Cinchy for Starters

**Size:** One size fits most

**Finished Measurements:** 56" long x 28" wide

**Materials:**

3 skeins Suss Mohair (76.5% mohair/17.5% wool/6% nylon; 42 grams /1.5 ounces; 102 yards/94 meters each), color sand

*LEFT: This poncho has become my signature look. I own about twenty in different yarns and colors. I travel with at least ten.*

2 skeins Suss Mohair (76.5% mohair/17.5% wool/6% nylon; 42 grams /1.5 ounces; 102 yards/94 meters each), color cream

2 skeins Suss Mohair (76.5% mohair/17.5% wool/6% nylon; 42 grams /1.5 ounces; 102 yards/94 meters each), color burgundy

1 pair size 15 (10mm) needles, or size to obtain gauge

1 size G/6 (4mm) crochet hook or larger

Tapestry needle

**Gauge:** 12 stitches and 16 rows = 4"/10 cm

## How to Knit:

Using sand, (leaving an 8" to 9" tail to be used for fringe later), cast on 84 stitches.

Begin Stockinette stitch (knit one right side row and purl one wrong side row), working in Stripe pattern as follows:

*Work 18 rows in sand–approximately 4 1/2".

Work 14 rows in cream–approximately 3 1/2".

Work 10 rows in burgundy–approximately 2 1/2".

Repeat from * for Stripe pattern, a total of 5 times–210 rows.

Work 18 rows in sand–228 rows total.

Bind off all stitches–piece measures approximately 56" from the beginning.

**Finishing:** Fold piece in half (see diagram). With wrong sides facing each other, seam one side together, beginning at the corner where the cast on edge and bound off edge meet (see diagram), leaving 11" opening on each side of fold line for head.

Fringe: Using the remaining yarn, cut 18" lengths for fringe. Using 2 lengths of yarn held together, attach fringe as follows:

Fold each group in half; using the crochet hook, pull one group through the lower edge of the Poncho, form a loop and pull ends through the loop; continue to add fringe at 1 1/2" intervals along the lower edge.

# vintage cap
## with rib

I MADE THIS CAP for the sailors in *Master and Commander: The Far Side of the World*, a movie starring Russell Crowe based on Patrick O'Brian's best-selling novels about life in the British navy during the Napoleonic wars. When my husband was reading the books, I had no idea I would be making nearly thirty hats for the movie.

The cap's old-fashioned look comes from the rib at the bottom and the loops on top and side—the loops allowed sailors to hang their caps on a nail on the wall at bedtime. I chose a durable, soft taupe–gray yarn because it's very basic and appropriate for the time period. Guys seem to love the color, which is easy to wear because it's solid and neutral.

**Experience Level:** Cinchy for Starters

**Size:** One size fits most

**Finished Measurements:** 7" long x 9" wide

**Materials:**

2 skeins Suss Ull (100% wool; 2 ounces/57 gram; 215 yards/198 meters), color ash

1 pair size 10 (6mm) needles, or size to obtain gauge

1 pair size 8 (5mm) needles, or size to obtain gauge

3 stitch holders

Tapestry needle

1 size G/6 (4mm) crochet hook

**Gauge:**

16 stitches and 24 rows = 4"/10 cm in Stockinette stitch using larger needles

24 stitches and 32 rows = 4"/10cm in 1x1 Rib using smaller needles

**How to Knit:**

Using two strands of yarn held together and smaller needles, cast on 72 stitches.

Work even in 1x1 Rib for 10 rows as follows:

LEFT: *Langston Fishburne is as handsome as his dad, Laurence, especially when he's wearing this sailor's cap.*

Row 1: *Knit 1, purl 1; repeat from *across.

Row 2: Knit the knit stitches and purl the purl stitches as they face you.

Repeat Rows 1 and 2 for 1x1 Rib—piece measures approximately 1 1/2".

(Right side): Change to larger needles and begin Stockinette stitch (knit one right side row and purl one wrong side row); work even until piece measures 5" from the beginning, ending after a right side row.

Dividing row: Divide the 72 stitches into 4 groups of 18 stitches; place each of 3 groups on individual stitch holders.

Continuing in Stockinette stitch, work 4 rows even on remaining group.

Shape Crown: Decrease 1 stitch on each side of this row. Work 2 rows even.

Decrease 1 stitch on each side of this row, then decrease 1 stitch on each side of every row for a total of 7 times until 1 stitch remains. Cut yarn and pull tail through last stitch to secure. Repeat shaping on remaining 3 groups of stitches.

**Finishing:** Weave in ends.

Fold knitted piece in half, right sides together, matching V-shaped edges. With the tapestry needle, sew along one V-shape at a time, then sew the back seam (see diagram).

Loops: Using the crochet hook, work a loop as follows: Work 8 chain stitches. Sew chain to top of the hat, forming a loop. Work a second loop in the same manner and sew to the seam of the hat.

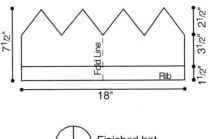

7 1/2"

Fold Line

Rib

18"

1/2" 3 1/2" 2 1/2"

Finished hat viewed from top

# variegated
# throw rug

**BELIEVE IT OR NOT,** this pattern is based on a classic knitted potholder design. It's a simple garter-stitch rectangle, worked tightly, with two colors of cotton yarn at a time. By changing colors, you get an interesting variegated look. When I was young, my mom made a round plastic version of this rug and I used to dance on it to music from the TV until I'd get dizzy. This is my new version—a tribute to my mom and our laughing together at my craziness.

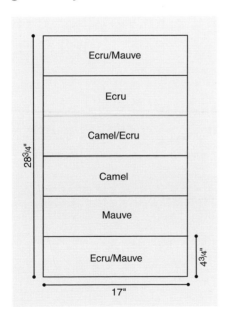

**Experience Level:** Cinchy for Starters

**Finished Measurements:**

28³/₄" long x 17" wide (without fringe)

LEFT: *I like to have lots of throw rugs on hand to change the look of a room in an instant.*

**Materials:**

3 skeins Suss Bomull (100% cotton; 4 ounces/114 grams; 190 yards/175 meters), color ecru

2 skeins Suss Bomull (100% cotton; 4 ounces/114 grams; 190 yards/175 meters), color camel

2 skeins Suss Bomull (100% cotton; 4 ounces/114 grams; 190 yards/175 meters), color mauve

1 pair size 8 (5mm) needles, or size to obtain gauge

1 size G/6 (4mm) crochet hook

**Gauge:** 12 stitches and 20 rows = 4"/10cm

**How to Knit:** Using 1 strand each of ecru and mauve held together, cast on 52 stitches.

Working in Garter stitch (knit every row) for entire length, work 24 rows using ecru and mauve—approximately 4³/₄".

Cut the ecru yarn; join another strand of mauve (so you have a double strand of mauve); work 24 rows.

Join a double strand of camel; work 24 rows.

Cut 1 strand of camel, join a strand of ecru; work 24 rows.

Change to a double strand of ecru; work 24 rows.

Cut 1 strand of ecru, add a strand of mauve; work 24 rows—144 rows total.

Bind off all stitches—piece measures 28³/₄" from the beginning.

**Finishing:** Weave in ends.

Fringe: Cut 76 strands of ecru yarn and 76 strands of mauve yarn, each 12" long.

Combine 2 strands of ecru with 2 strands of mauve for each group—38 groups of fringe.

Fold each group in half; using the crochet hook, pull one group through the edge of the rug, form a loop and pull ends through the loop. Attach fringe to both ends, spacing them 1" apart.

# monogrammed
# kid's sweater

**THE GARNET HILL CATALOGUE** carried this design for a long time. Monogrammed in a contrast color, it's my favorite gift for my friends' children. Included is a diagram for you to embroider the appropriate initial. In fact, I've included all the letters of the alphabet—you can embroider the whole name if you want. I found these Swedish letters from the Gustavian period in an old book. In the past, they were often embroidered on hand towels in Sweden.

LEFT: *Layla Gold, my niece, always looks "D for Darling."*
ABOVE: *To make the monogram, photocopy and enlarge the letter you want from page 35, then pin the paper right to the sweater and embroider over it. When you're done embroidering, simply tear the paper away.*

**Experience Level:** Step Up and Knit

**Sizes:** 2 (4, 6) years

**Finished Measurements:**

Chest: 28 (30, 32)"

Length: 14 (15, 17)"

**Materials:**

3 (3, 4) skeins Suss Bomull (100% cotton; 4 ounces/ 114 grams; 190 yards/175 meters), color naturale

1 pair size 8 (5mm) needles, or size to obtain gauge

1 size 7 (4.5mm) circular needle, 16"/40cm long

2 stitch holders

Tapestry needle

**Gauge:** 16 stitches and 24 rows = 4"/10cm

**How to Knit:**

**BACK**

Cast on 56 (60, 64) stitches.

Begin Stockinette stitch (knit one right side row and purl one wrong side row); work even until piece measures 13 (14, 16)" from the beginning, ending after a wrong side row.

Shape shoulders: Bind off 8 (8, 6) stitches each side every other row for a total of 2 (2, 3) times—24 (28, 28) stitches remain.

Place the remaining stitches on a stitch holder for neck.

**FRONT**

Cast on 56 (60, 64) stitches.

Work even in Stockinette stitch as for Back until piece measures

10 1/2 (11 1/2, 13 1/2)" from the beginning, ending after a wrong side row.

Shape left neck: Work across 22 (24, 26) stitches; place the center 12 stitches on a stitch holder for neck; place the remaining 22 (24, 26) stitches on another stitch holder.

At the neck edge, bind off 2 stitches every other row for a total of 1 (2, 2) times–20 (20, 22) stitches remain.

Decrease 1 stitch at the neck edge every other row for a total of 4 times–16 (16, 18) stitches remain for shoulder.

Work even until piece measures same as Back to Shoulder shaping, ending after a wrong side row.

Shape shoulder: At armhole edge, bind off 8 (8, 6) stitches every other row for a total of 2 (2, 3) times.

Work right neck and shoulder as for left, reversing all shaping; leave center stitches on holder for neck.

### SLEEVES

Cast on 28 (28, 30) stitches; begin Stockinette stitch.

Shape sleeve: Increase 1 stitch on each side every 8 (7, 7) rows for a total of 7 (9, 10) times–42 (46, 50) stitches. Work even until piece measures 10 (11, 12)" from the beginning; bind off the remaining stitches.

Make a second sleeve the same as the first.

### COLLAR

Place Front and Back pieces together with right sides facing each other. Using a tapestry needle and yarn, sew shoulder seams together, matching bound off rows.

Using the circular needle, beginning at the left shoulder seam, pick up and knit 32 stitches around the Front neck shaping (including the 12 stitches from the stitch holder), and the 24 (28, 28) stitches from the Back neck stitch holder–56 (60, 60) stitches. Knit evenly around neck opening for 12 rows– approximately 3".

Bind off all stitches.

### Finishing:

Weave in ends.

Sew side seam, beginning at lower edge and ending 8 (8 1/2, 10)" from the lower edge for the beginning of the armhole.

Fold sleeves lengthwise, right sides facing each other, and sew sleeve seams.

Sew sleeves into armholes.

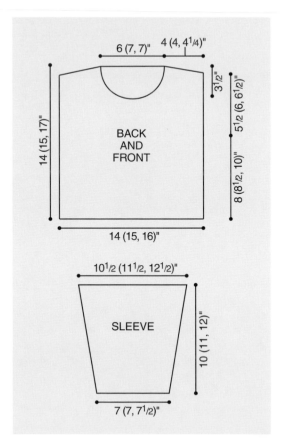

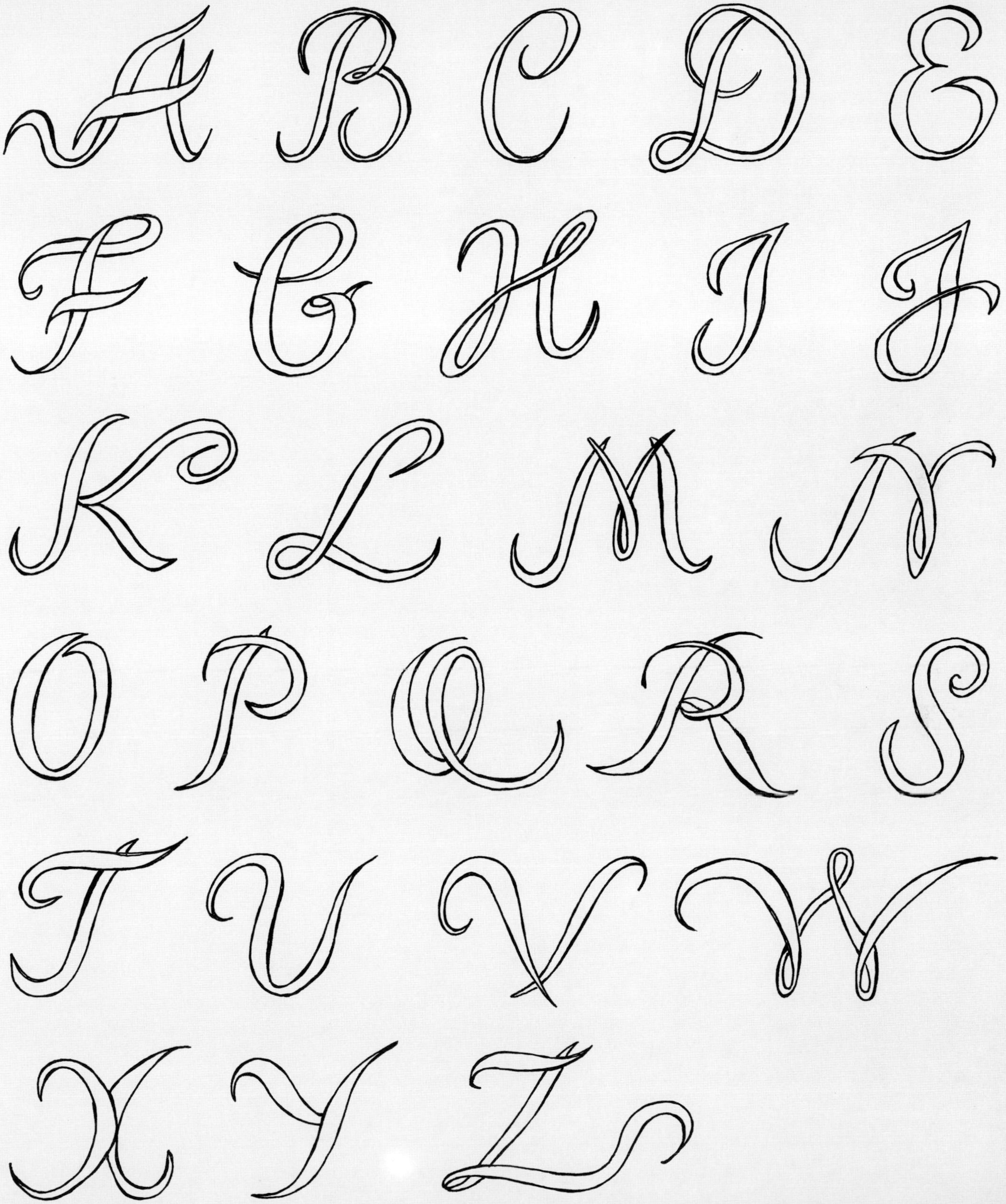

A B C D E

F G H I J

K L M N

O P Q R S

T U V W

X Y Z

# (CHAPTER 2)
# the knitting life

THE ACT OF KNITTING IS A RELAXING and pleasurable pastime, but the finished product is what gives us a sense of accomplishment. For the sake of both, it's good to incorporate knitting into your busy everyday life. People who don't knit for a living like me might think it is difficult to find the time. But the great thing about knitting is that it's portable and can be picked up and put down at your convenience. It can be done practically anywhere, even when you've got to stay focused on something else. Don't think of it as another time-eater; think of it as a fabulous way to enrich your time.

## Finding Time and Space

The best way to find time to knit? Don't leave the house without your knitting! You never know when you might have a few minutes to spare while sitting in the waiting room at the doctor's office, waiting for your child to finish a rehearsal, or getting stuck in traffic (that happens to me a lot, living in Los Angeles!). I once heard about a woman who knit her way through labor, but that seems a little extreme, even to a passionate knitter like me.

Another general rule of knitting is to keep a project anywhere you're likely to plop down and have a window of opportunity. For example, if you keep a small, simple piece of knitting next to your computer you can knit while waiting for Internet downloads or for friends to instant-message.

My favorite place to knit is in bed, so I always keep a knitting bag there. The most relaxing thing I can think of is to put on comfortable clothes, puff up my pillows, and sink into them with my knitting. Often one of my daughters will come sit with me, and we'll watch a movie together.

I frequently see people knitting while waiting in line. One time I was stuck at the Department of Motor Vehicles for two hours. I saw three people knitting. For some reason, I hadn't brought my knitting with me that day, and it was torture. Knitting makes time pass quickly when you're waiting and can be relaxing in frustrating situations. Also, when you knit in public, you tend to attract attention, so it becomes a great conversation starter.

Knitting during a commute is practical if you take a train or bus. No matter how long your ride, knitting will make it seem shorter. Maybe you'll look forward to your long commute if you have something productive to do during it! Another good place to knit is on a plane. I've heard of some people having their needles confiscated because of security concerns, so I always bring wooden needles (instead of metal or plastic) because they don't seem to set off any alarms. I also put my needles in a case as an extra precaution. Almost everytime I travel to New York I make a scarf and hat and get off the plane feeling warm and cozy.

A lot of people tell me that they like to knit during their lunch hour. They eat first, then knit instead of reading or smoking. Knitting is also a fantastic stress reliever. Several actresses I know take their knitting to auditions to help them stay calm. Knitting before a meeting or presentation definitely soothes the nerves. Sometimes I even knit during my business meetings. But those meetings are usually related to knitting in some way, so it's very natural. Knitting in low-key meetings like school assemblies or big lecture classes is usually fine.

A great way to wind down on the weekends is to go to a coffeehouse and knit. I see it all the time: People sit there with a cup of coffee and their projects just grow and grow. Something about the combination of the smell of the coffee and the act of knitting is wonderful. In Swedish, we call that feeling *gemytligt.*

## Knitting Etiquette

Use your judgment when deciding whether or not to knit in any given situation. If in doubt, always ask politely for permission. I definitely would not knit during an important meeting or in a fancy restaurant. If you want to knit in a class, first ask your professor if it's okay. Although I think knitting in church is fine, some of your fellow parishioners may not agree. If a train or a bus is particularly crowded, resist the urge to knit to avoid inadvertently poking someone with a sharp needle. Nevertheless, remember that in most contexts, people will be impressed and intrigued by your knitting rather than bothered by it.

## Kids Knitting

Knitting is a wonderful way to introduce children to a new skill and a tradition. It can also keep them from watching too much television or getting involved in some less wholesome activities. One day a woman came into my store with five little girls and this concept really came to life for me. She explained that she and four other moms had started a group called School Girls, for which each mother takes a turn teaching the girls a skill—cooking, drawing, knitting, etc. This woman wanted to show the girls how I had created a business based on knitting. I was thrilled she had chosen me as a role model, and spent the afternoon showing them baby clothes, giving them some nice yarn to practice on, and teaching them to finger-knit.

You can introduce kids to knitting at a fairly young age. My six-year-old, Viveka, can always be counted on to lend a running commentary about my knitting at home. "It's growing. It's growing," she'll say, as I hold up a scarf to show her my progress. She doesn't knit yet, but her enthusiasm is so infectious, we came up with a way for her

ABOVE: *My mom handknit these doll clothes and sent them to me when my daughter Viveka was born.*

to approximate actual knitting using only her fingers: We loosely tie the yarn around her finger and she makes continuous little knots using both index fingers as if they were knitting needles. She made a choker this way, and decorated it with beads. And, oh, is she ever proud to wear that choker she knit herself! I also taught Viveka's class at school how to finger-knit. Everyone loved it, even the boys. You might try this with your young child who doesn't have the patience or dexterity yet to begin knitting for real. My older daughter, Hanna, was focused enough and eager to learn to knit at age seven. Definitely encourage kids when they're young.

## The Art of Handmade Giving

I love knitting gifts for my friends. Giving people something handknit is the most personal kind of gift. Sweaters are generally the hardest to make since you have to know a person pretty well to get the dimensions right. I'm good at guessing my friends' sizes, but if you're not confident about doing this and you want to make it a surprise, it's best to give one-size projects like scarves, hats, wraps, or ponchos. Also, before you start, make sure that you know whether your friend is allergic to any fibers, such as wool or angora. I've had to think up some sneaky ways to find this out without my friends catching on. Once a project is done, I like to add a few finishing touches to make the item really special.

A monogram, for example, makes a gift unique and extra-personal. When my friend Kelly's daughter was a newborn I knitted her a jacket and embroidered her name on the back. She's had it forever; a monogrammed piece really touches the recipient's heart, I think.

When I give a handknit gift, sometimes I tuck in a little extra something that I didn't make, like a coordinating tie, nail polish, scarf, or pair of earrings. This icing on the knit cake is sure to delight the lucky person.

## creative gift wraps

Wrapping is my favorite part of the present process. It's a way to add your last touches of creativity and make your gift complete.

**YARN BOWS:** Even if you're just using regular wrapping paper, make it extra special with a little bit of leftover yarn to tie up the package. Use several strands of the yarn that was used to make your gift or yarn that complements its colors. For a bit of sparkle, twist some gold or silver thread with the strands.

**HANDMADE BAGS:** I love to give gifts in little bags I've made of chiffon or velvet. Just take two equal-sized squares of fabric and sew three sides together. Fold the fourth edge of each square over and stitch it down, making a little tunnel to thread a ribbon through. Insert the ribbon and pull through so that you have a drawstring. Then turn this "bag" inside out so that the stitching is not visible. This is how I most often give gifts; it's so easy and cute!

**THEMED PACKAGING:** Use the gift itself as inspiration for your packaging. If you're giving someone the Travel Blanket Set (page 50), use an old map for wrapping paper. Package baby booties in a diaper bag or tie a pacifier into the bow. For a monogrammed sweater or a scarf, try monogramming the card or even the box with the same thread.

## music to click by

My husband put together this selection of great music for me to play in the store for knitting nights. It's as eclectic as can be, but it seems to help everyone get in the perfect mood for knitting and socializing.

**Sweet Lorraine**
NAT KING COLE

**Ce Que L'On Tait**
AUTOUR DE LUCIE

**Little Eyes**
YO LA TENGO

**On Your Side**
PETE YORN

**You've Made Me So Very Happy**
BLOOD SWEAT & TEARS

**Que Lueva!**
JUANA MOLINA

**California**
JONI MITCHELL

**Women's Realm**
BELLE AND SEBASTIAN

# little labels

Putting labels on your finished projects gives them an added creative touch and professional finish. Just imagine your friends showing off their new sweaters and pointing out your signature label! Alternatively, some knitters I know have used labels to write their own message to the wearer, like "Love, Cindy." Over the years, I've gone through many different styles of labels for my own creations. I even offer a class on finishing and labeling. A note of caution: never write directly on the yarn because it will bleed and look sloppy.

**RUBBER STAMPS:** Instead of writing on labels with a pen, I stamp them with a rubber stamp. At many big copy shops  you can get a personalized stamp with your name for about $10. If you buy good ink, the stamp will stay on the label for many washes.

**LEATHER LABELS:** I once did an adorable heart-shaped label out of leather. Cut a small piece of leather in any shape you like. Use a stamp or a good black pen to write your name on it. Punch holes around the edges of the leather with a sewing needle and then sew it into the project.

**RIBBON LABELS:** Fabric ribbon labels are wonderful because they are both cheap and chic. You can buy different colors of ribbon to go with different yarns. Stamp them, write on them with pen, or embroider them. Then fold over both short ends and sew them onto the project with thread of a contrasting color.

**KNIT LABELS:** You can knit a small swatch and use it as a label. Choose a color that contrasts with the yarn you used to knit the item. Then embroider your name or a special message on it.

**EMBROIDERY:** If your project is made out of a thicker, thightly knit yarn, you can embroider a label right onto it (make sure that the embroidery does not show through to the other side). I like to do this with thin gold thread for an elegant effect.

**IRON-ON AND SEW-IN CLOTHING LABELS:** This is the simplest way to label your clothing. You can order as few as 20 at a time online and write or stamp on them. Try www.prontolabels.com to order online.

(A KNIT AFFAIR)

# getaway knitting
# night

### Occasion/Theme

A party to plan vacations with the help of your friends—while you knit.
Invite everyone to bring travel brochures, photos of places they've visited
in the past, and plenty of maps.

### Time/Season

A weekday dinner, around mid-March, after the winter holiday whirl.

### Project

Knit the Travel Blanket Set (page 50); it works as a pillow and/or a blanket
in a soft lush yarn. It's an easy pattern, so you don't have to spend time
figuring out too many stitches (concentrate on those pictures of white sandy
beaches and bright blue oceans instead).

### Music

Music from destinations you are considering: steel drums, African beat,
Parisian café songs.

### Variations

Make it a post-vacation gathering at the end of the summer or beginning
of fall. Guests bring photos or videos of their trips and everyone knits a new
scarf for the changing season. A way to ease the end-of-vacation slump!

## menu

**Lingonberry Delight
or Sparkling Pear Cider**

**Small Swedish
Meatballs**

**Swedish Pancakes**

(all recipes on page 137)

# everything
## bag

A FEW YEARS AGO, I MADE A BAG like this for a movie called *ID*. I think this version is so chic with its funky textural yarn and matching pink denim lining; it's also roomy enough to be quite practical—makes a good weekend bag, in fact. The braided suede handles allow it to go over your shoulder easily, without feeling stiff. I also love the huge wooden button on the pocket—it's a great detail that contrasts with the leather.

**Experience Level:** Cinchy for Starters

**Finished Measurements:**

15" long x 22" wide (lower edge); 18" wide (top edge)

**Materials:**

8 skeins Suss Charm (50% cotton/ 50% nylon; 2 ounces/ 115 grams; 93 yards/86 meters each), color mauve/chocolate

1 pair size 10 (6mm) needles, or size to obtain gauge

1 size G/6 (4mm) crochet hook

Tapestry needle

LEFT: *Use this roomy bag to hold anything and everything—yoga clothes, swimsuit and towel, even diapers travel in style.*

Sewing needle

Thread to match yarn

1 pair suede braided handles (available from Suss Design, see page 134)

1 button (7/8" diameter)

Hot pink denim fabric–23" wide x 36" long (for lining)

Thread to match lining fabric

**Gauge:**

12 stitches and 16 rows = 4"/10 cm in Stockinette stitch

**How to Knit:**

Back and Front (both alike): Cast on 66 stitches.

Work even in Stockinette stitch (knit one right side row and purl one wrong side row) for 10 rows, ending after a wrong side row.

Shape sides: Decrease 1 stitch on each side this row, then every 10 rows for a total of 5 times–56 stitches remain.

Work even until piece measures 15" from the beginning.

Bind off all stitches.

Patch Pocket (make 1): Cast on 21 stitches.

Work even in Stockinette stitch for 26 rows–piece measures 6 1/2" from the beginning.

Bind off all stitches.

**Finishing:**

Pocket: Center pocket on Front piece, 15 rows up from the cast on (lower) edge.

Using tapestry needle and yarn, whipstitch 3 sides of pocket onto piece (see diagram).

Using sewing needle and thread, sew button onto top center edge of pocket.

Using the crochet hook, insert hook into center of Front above pocket; work a chain approximately 3" long; form loop by pulling end through the beginning stitch (see schematic).

Place Front and Back pieces together, with right sides facing each other.

Using tapestry needle and yarn, beginning at lower edge, sew sides together, stopping 3" from top edge.

Sew lower edge seam.

Handles: Fold 2" of the upper edge (bound off edge) of one piece over a braided handle.

Using sewing needle and thread, whipstitch into place. Repeat for second handle.

Turn piece right side out.

Lining: Cut lining fabric to shape (see diagram). Fold lining in half, with right sides facing each other; pin sides together.

Using sewing needle and thread, sew sides together, stopping 3" from top edge of lining. Do not turn right side out.

Place lining inside purse, turn upper edge to wrong side and sew into place along top edges, covering seams where handles were attached; allow fabric to gather along handles as necessary.

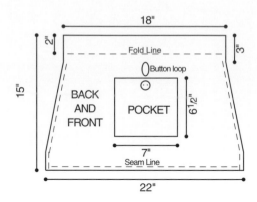

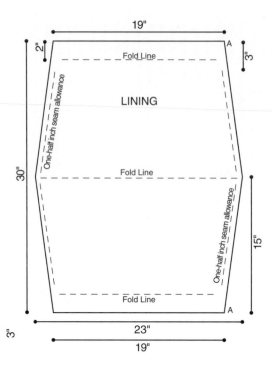

# his and her
# dog sweaters

ONE DAY THE DOG WHO STARRED in the movie *Cats and Dogs* came to the store (with his trainer). My daughter happened to be there and, of course, she fell totally in love with the dog, which made me think about how people get attached to their animals. So I thought I would start making a few items for man's (and woman's) best friend. I picked sophisticated rather than cute colors for these topstitched doggy sweaters. The Aspen yarn stretches, which makes it easy and fast to knit. And, of course, the yarn is washable so if your little pup gets into any messy mischief, it's not a problem to clean.

**Experience Level:** Cinchy for Starters

**Size:** One size fits smaller dogs

**Finished Measurements:**

15³/₄" long x 14¹/₂" circumference

**Materials [Hers(His)]:**

2 balls GGH Aspen (50% wool/50% acrylic; 1.75 ounces/ 50 grams; 62 yards/57 meters each), color #29 lavender (#35 light teal)

1 ball GGH Aspen (50% wool/50% acrylic; 1.75 ounces/ 50 grams; 62 yards/57 meters each), color #6 burgundy (#37 light yellow)

1 pair size 13 (9mm) needles, or size to obtain gauge

1 size G/6 (4mm) crochet hook

**Gauge:**

12 stitches and 16 rows – 4"/10 cm in Stockinette stitch

**How to Knit:**

Note: Sweater is worked in two pieces, right and left sides, then crocheted together at center Back and Front.

## LEFT SIDE

Using color #29 lavender (#35 light teal), cast on 14 stitches.

Begin Stockinette stitch (knit one right side row and purl one wrong side row), beginning purl 1 row.

Shape Body: At center Front, increase 1 stitch at the beginning of this row, then every other row for a total of 8 times–22 stitches. (This will create shaping along the right-hand side of piece, while keeping the center Back straight.)

Work even through Row 33, ending after a wrong side row.

Row 34: Knit 4 stitches, bind off 5 stitches (along shaped side for leg opening), work to end.

Row 35: Purl across to bound off stitches, cast on 5 stitches above previously bound off stitches, work to end.

Work even through Row 43, ending after a wrong side row.

Shape Neck: Knit 4 stitches; decrease 6 stitches across the following 12 stitches by knitting 2 together 6 times; work to end—16 stitches remain.

Work even for 20 rows.

Bind off remaining stitches.

### RIGHT SIDE

Work as for Left side, reversing all shaping.

## Finishing:

Weave in ends.

Place pieces together with wrong sides facing each other.

Using the crochet hook and #6 burgundy (#37 light yellow), single crochet pieces together along center Back, then single crochet along center Front (see diagram).

Work 1 row of single crochet around leg openings and neck openings and bottom edge.

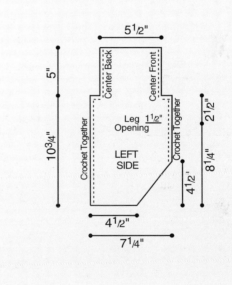

*LEFT: My assistant Yoshie's dogs Chewi and Indy are so cute; they didn't even mind modeling their sweaters.*

# travel
# blanket set

BETWEEN BUSINESS AND KEEPING UP with friends and family, I fly quite often, but I don't like those uncomfortable airline blankets and pillows. So I came up with a travel set in a lush angora mix. Use the blanket in the bag as a pillow; or cuddle up under the blanket on its own. The tonal edging is slightly conservative; change to a contrasting color for a bolder effect. Or add a monogram if you want this blanket to look like the one I made for *InStyle* magazine. It seems we never outgrow wanting our very own blankies!

**Experience Level:** Cinchy for Starters

## Finished Measurements:

Blanket: 50" long x 30" wide

Bag: 8" long x 16" wide

## Materials:

10 skeins Classic Elite's Lush (50% angora/50% wool; 1.75 ounces/ 50 grams; 124 yards/114 meters), color #4438 camel

1 skein Classic Elite's Lush (50% angora/50% wool; 1.75 ounces/ 50 grams; 124 yards/114 meters), color #4476 chocolate brown

LEFT: *Try making this blanket set in bulky cotton for a great kid's sleep-over accessory.*

1 pair size 9 (5.5mm) needles, or size to obtain gauge

1 pair size 8 (5mm) needles, or size to obtain gauge

1 size G/6 (4mm) crochet hook

Tapestry needle

## Gauge:

16 stitches and 20 rows = 4"/10 cm in Stockinette stitch using larger needles (blanket)

20 stitches and 24 rows = 4"/10cm in Stockinette using smaller needles (bag)

## How to Knit:

### BLANKET

Using larger needles and camel, cast on 120 stitches.

Work even in Stockinette stitch (knit one right side row and purl one wrong side row) until piece measures 50" from the beginning.

Bind off all stitches. Block with steam to flatten edges and even out stitches.

## Finishing:

Edging: Using the crochet hook and chocolate brown, work 1 row of single crochet around entire blanket. (Note: Work 3 stitches into the same stitch in each corner to round off nicely.)

### BAG

Using smaller needles and camel, cast on 80 stitches.

Work even in Stockinette stitch (knit one right side row and purl one wrong side row) until piece measures 26" from the beginning.

Bind off all stitches.

## Finishing:

Place a marker 8" up from cast on edge at each side (lower fold line). With right sides facing each other, fold the cast on edge of the piece up to the second fold line (point A to point A; see diagram) at markers. Sew 8" side seams, beginning at fold and working up. Turn bag right side out.

Edging: Using the crochet hook and chocolate brown, work 1 row of single crochet around 3 sides of flap. (Note: Work 3 stitches into the same stitch in each corner to round off nicely.) Place a marker at the center of flap (bound off edge), and at the center of fold at lower edge.

Ties: Using the crochet hook, work a chain 10" long; do not fasten off. Join chain to the flap at the marker with a single crochet stitch; fasten off. Work a second 10" chain and attach it to the center of the folded edge.

Fold flap down (bound off edge to folded lower edge) and tie a bow to close bag.

Strap: Cut 15 strands of yarn, each 35" long. Tie strands together with an overhand knot at one end; divide strands into 3 groups of 5 strands each and braid; secure end with an overhand knot. Sew strap onto outside of bag at side seams.

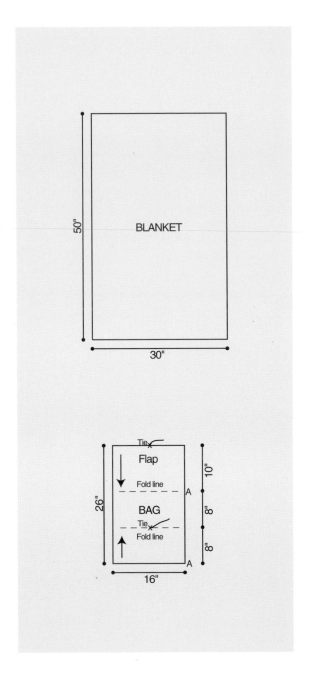

# red riding
## hood scarf

**I FIRST MADE THIS HOODED SCARF** in cream, but when I tried it on, I realized that I felt just like Little Red Riding Hood, so I had to have it in red Suss Lash. If you don't close the wooden buttons in the back of the head piece, it becomes a regular scarf. The bottom is shaped to hang longer in the front.

**Experience Level:** Step Up and Knit

**Finished Measurements:**

85½" long, 13¼" wide (hood), 10" wide (scarf)

**Materials:**

8 balls Suss Lash (60% cotton/40% nylon; 2 ounces/57 grams; 67 yards/62 meters each), color red

1 pair size 10 (6mm) needles, or size to obtain gauge

1 size G/6 (4mm) crochet hook

Sewing needle

Three buttons, ⅞"–1" diameter

**Gauge:**

12 stitches and 16 rows = 4"/10 cm in Stockinette stitch

**How to Knit:**

Cast on 3 stitches.

Begin Stockinette stitch (knit one right side row and purl one wrong side row), beginning purl 1 row.

Shape end: Cast on 3 stitches at the beginning of this row, then every other row for a total of 9 times–30 stitches.

Work even for 100 rows, ending after a wrong side row.

Shape hood section: Increase 1 stitch on each side every other row for a total of 5 times–40 stitches; piece measures 32" from beginning, measured along longest side.

Work even for 86 rows, ending after a wrong side row.

Decrease 1 stitch on each side every other row for a total of 5 times–30 stitches remaining.

Work even for 100 rows, ending after a wrong side row.

Shape End: Bind off 3 stitches at beginning of this row, then every other row for a total of 10 times–no stitches remain.

## Finishing:

Weave in ends.

Fold scarf in half. On center section, along the longer edge of the scarf (see diagram), place markers for button and button loop placements, 3½", 7" and 10½" each side of center fold.

Edging and button loops: Using the crochet hook, beginning on longer edge, work in single crochet to first button loop marker, work button loops as follows:

When you reach the loop marker: *Chain 11, slip stitch into the last single crochet worked (one loop completed); repeat from * for 2 remaining loops, continuing to work single crochet along edge between loops.

When loops are completed, continue working 1 row of single crochet around remaining edges; fasten off. (Note: Work 3 stitches into the same stitch in each corner to round off nicely.)

Sew buttons at markers, approximately 1" from finished edge.

## Fringe:

Cut 32 strands of yarn, each 20" long.

Combine 2 strands of yarn for each fringe (16 groups).

Fold each group in half; using the crochet hook, pull one group through the end of the scarf, form a loop and pull ends through the loop. Attach 8 fringes to each end of scarf, evenly spaced.

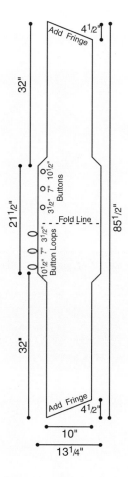

LEFT: *A fairy-tale scarf for a fairy-tale girl.*

# magic
# wrap

YOU MAY HAVE SEEN THIS unusual wrap, one of my most unique pieces, in the Anthropologie catalogue. It's shaped almost like a vest and has a button closure, but it drapes like a shawl. I think costume designer Rita Ryack looks incredibly sophisticated wearing it with a soft blouse and A-line skirt. I call the beautiful mix of Twisted, Lash, Ull, Bomull, and Mohair my Suss Magic Yarn!

**Experience Level:** Step Up and Knit

**Size:** One size fits most

**Finished Measurements:** 30" long x 52" wide

LEFT: *Talented costume designer Rita Ryack wears my knitwear especially well. She's an inspiration!*

## Materials:

2 skeins Suss Twisted (100% slub cotton; 4 ounces/ 114 grams; 184 yards/169 meters each), color moss green/sage

2 skeins Suss Lash (60% cotton/40% nylon; 2 ounces/ 57 grams; 67 yards/62 meters each), color olive

3 skeins Suss Mohair (76.5% mohair/17.5% wool/6% nylon; 1.5 ounces/42 grams; 102 yards/94 meters each), color sand

2 skeins Suss Ull (100% wool; 2 ounces/57 grams/ 215 yards/198 meters each), color stone

2 skeins Suss Ull (100% wool; 2 ounces/57 grams/ 215 yards/198 meters each), color arctic moss

2 skeins Suss Bomull (100% cotton; 4 ounces/114 grams; 190 yards/175 meters each), color mauve

1 pair size 10 (6mm) needles, or size to obtain gauge

Tapestry needle

1 leather half-dome button (1 1/8" diameter)

## Gauge:

16 stitches and 20 rows = 4"/10 cm in Stockinette stitch

(Note: Gauge will vary due to the different weights of yarn used.)

## STRIPE SEQUENCE NOTES

Whenever Suss Ull appears in Stripe Sequence, use 2 strands of yarn held together.

Collar: Alternate colors of Stripe Sequence (see page 58) throughout the piece, beginning at * (308 rows total).

Body: Work in colors indicated for first 38 rows, then work Stripe Sequence, beginning at ** for the remainder of the piece (260 rows total).

Working in Stockinette stitch (knit one right side row and purl one wrong side row) throughout, work as follows:

## STRIPE SEQUENCE

*26 rows–Suss Bomull mauve

8 rows–Suss Ull arctic moss

14 rows–Suss Twisted moss green/sage

10 rows–Suss Lash olive

20 rows–Suss Mohair sand

8 rows–Suss Ull stone

**16 rows–Suss Bomull mauve

12 rows–Suss Ull arctic moss

24 rows–Suss Twisted moss green/sage

10 rows–Suss Lash olive

14 rows–Suss Mohair sand

20 rows–Suss Ull stone

10 rows–Suss Bomull mauve

16 rows–Suss Ull arctic moss

16 rows–Suss Twisted moss green/sage

10 rows–Suss Lash olive

20 rows–Suss Mohair sand

10 rows–Suss Ull stone

14 rows–Suss Bomull mauve

30 rows–Suss Ull arctic moss

## How to Knit:

### COLLAR

Using Suss Bomull mauve, cast on 3 stitches.

Work even in Stripe Sequence for 2 rows, ending after a wrong side row.

Shape Collar: (Right side) Cast on 3 stitches at the beginning of this row, then every other row for a total of 11 times–36 stitches. Work even in Stripe Sequence, ending with Row 50 of Stripe Sequence (2 rows of Suss Lash olive have been worked).

Buttonhole: Knit across to last 6 sts, bind off 2 stitches, work to end. Next row: Purl 4, cast on 2 stitches above bound off sts, work to end.

Work even until piece measures 57" from the beginning, measured along longer edge, ending with Row 284 of Stripe Sequence (6 rows of Suss Ull artic moss have been worked).

Shape Collar: Beginning this row, bind off 3 stitches every other row for a total of 11 times–3 stitches remaining. Purl 1 row even.

Bind off remaining stitches–piece measures 62" from the beginning, measured along longer edge; 52" along shorter edge.

## BODY

In Stockinette stitch, work in stripes as given below, then work from ** of Stripe Sequence to end:

12 rows–Suss Lash olive

20 rows–Suss Mohair sand

6 rows–Suss Ull stone

Using Suss Lash olive, cast on 3 stitches; work even in Stockinette stitch for 2 rows, ending after a wrong side row.

Shape Body: (Right side) Cast on 3 stitches at beginning of this row, then every other row for a total of 13 times–42 stitches.

Cast on 2 stitches every other row for a total of 14 times–70 stitches.

Increase 1 stitch every other row for a total of 10 times–80 stitches (76 rows completed).

Continuing in Stripe Sequence, work even until 184 rows have been completed.

Shape Body: (Right side) Decrease 1 stitch at the beginning of this row, then every other row for a total of 10 times–70 stitches remain.

Bind off 2 stitches every other row for a total of 14 times–42 stitches remain.

Bind off 3 stitches every other row for a total of 13 times–3 stitches remain. Purl 1 row even. Bind off remaining stitches– piece measures 52" in length, measured along longest edge.

## Finishing:

Weave in ends.

Lay Body piece flat on a table, wrong side facing, with the straight edge out in front of you. Place markers for armholes along straight edge as follows: Beginning at one end, place a marker 10" from edge; next marker 8" from previous marker (armhole); next marker 16" from previous marker (neck and shoulders); and final marker 8" from previous marker (armhole) –there is 10" remaining at opposite edge (see diagram).

Place the Collar piece flat on the table with the wrong side facing, its narrow edge up against the straight edge of the Body (see diagram).

Using tapestry needle and yarn of choice, sew pieces together, leaving 8 inch sections (armholes) unsewn.

After attaching the pieces, fold the wrap, aligning edges of Collar; mark placement for button (see diagram).

Sew button into place (see photo on page 56).

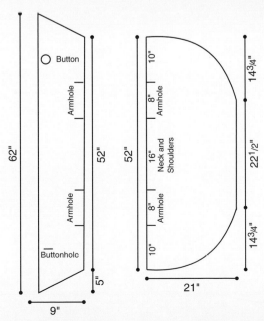

62"

52"

9"

5"

○ Button

Armhole

Armhole

Buttonhole

52"

10"

8"
Armhole

16"
Neck and
Shoulders

8"
Armhole

10"

21"

14³/₄"

22¹/₂"

14³/₄"

# cozy tweed
# cardigan

**WEAR THIS SWEATER YOUR OWN WAY**—on the shoulders for classic style or off the shoulders for a sexy, natural look. In a soft, organic-looking wool, it reminds me of the costumes in a movie from the 1980s called *Escape from New York*. The closure is a pin that I made by wrapping a knitting needle in leather and capping it with a natural stone—very earthy.

**Experience Level:** Step Up and Knit

**Size:** One chest size fits most

Note: Three body and sleeve lengths are given in instructions.

**Finished Measurements:**

Chest: 42" all sizes

Length: 21 (22, 23)"

**Materials:**

7 (7, 8) skeins Suss Speckled (90% wool/10% cotton; 2 ounces/57 grams; 114 yards/104 meters each), color oatmeal

1 pair size 10 (6mm) needles, or size to obtain gauge

Tapestry needle

Pin for closure

**Gauge:**

16 stitches and 20 rows = 4"/10 cm in Stockinette stitch

## How to Knit:

### BACK

Cast on 84 stitches.

Work even in Stockinette stitch (knit one right side row and purl one wrong side row) until piece measures 13 (14, 15)" from the beginning, ending after a wrong side row.

Shape armhole (dropped sleeve): Cast on 12 stitches at the beginning of the next 2 rows–108 stitches.

Work even until piece measures 7" from armhole shaping, ending after a wrong side row.

*LEFT: Anna Jonsson, a Swedish model and friend from New York, in a cardigan you will want to wear all the time.*

Shape shoulders: At each side, bind off 8 stitches 4 times, 9 stitches on each side once–26 stitches remain for neck.

Bind off remaining stitches.

## LEFT FRONT

Cast on 56 stitches.

Work even in Stockinette stitch until piece measures 10 (11, 12)" from the beginning, ending after a right side row.

Shape neck: At the neck edge, decrease 1 stitch every other row 27 times, WHILE AT THE SAME TIME, when the piece measures the same length as the Back to armhole shaping—13 (14, 15)"—end after a wrong side row.

Shape armhole (dropped sleeve): Cast on 12 stitches at beginning of row, work to end.

Continuing neck shaping, work until piece measures the same as the Back to shoulder shaping, ending after a wrong side row.

Shape shoulder as for Back (at armhole edge, bind off 8 stitches 4 times, 9 stitches once).

## RIGHT FRONT

Work as for Left Front, reversing all shaping.

## SLEEVES

Sew shoulder seams as follows:

Place Front and Back pieces together, right sides facing each other.

Using a tapestry needle and yarn, sew shoulder seams together, matching shaping.

With right side facing, pick up and knit 54 stitches along armhole (dropped sleeve) edge, 27 stitches from the Front, 27 stitches from the Back; begin Stockinette stitch.

WHILE AT THE SAME TIME,

Shape sleeve: Decrease 1 stitch each side every 9 rows 8 times –38 stitches remain.

Work even until piece measures 16 (17, 18)" from the beginning (pick up row).

Bind off remaining stitches.

### Finishing:

Weave in ends.

With right sides facing each other, sew side and sleeve seams, beginning at the lower edge and continuing along sleeve, ending at wrist edge.

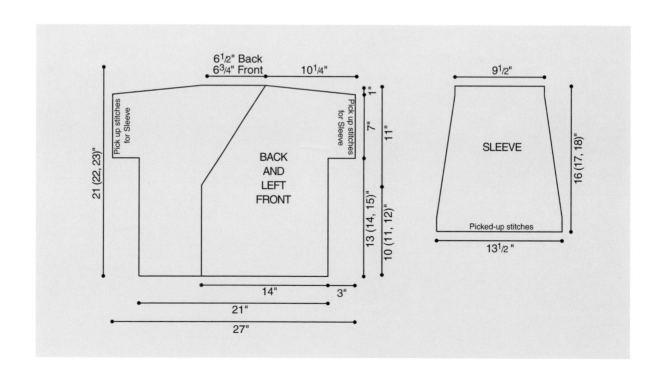

# bohemian
## skirt

**I SOLD THIS SKIRT TO ALL THE STORES** that carry my ready-to-wear designs. I decided to include it in this book after I spotted it on a girl leaving the charming Ivy restaurant in Los Angeles and saw how cute it looked. I think this piece will have a long life because it's classic, but the fringe gives it a bit of an edge. In a neutral olive shade with a braid around the waist, the skirt sits low on your hip.

**Experience Level:** Step Up and Knit

**Sizes:** Extra-Small (Small, Medium, Large)

**Finished Measurements:**

Hip:  27 (29, 31, 33)"

Length: 23 (24, 25, 26)"

**Materials:**

3 (3, 4, 4) skeins Suss Spacedye (100% cotton; 4 ounces/ 114 grams; 190 yards/175 meters each), color earthtone

1 skein Suss Bomull (100% cotton; 4 ounces/114 grams; 190 yards/175 meters each), color olive

1 pair size 9 (5.5mm) needles, or size to obtain gauge

1 size J/10 (6mm) crochet hook

Tapestry needle

**Gauge:**

16 stitches and 20 rows = 4"/10 cm in Stockinette stitch

**How to Knit:**

### FRONT AND BACK (BOTH ALIKE)

Using olive, cast on 48 (52, 56, 60) stitches, leaving a 4"–5" tail.

Work in Stockinette stitch (knit one right side row and purl one wrong side row), beginning purl 1 row.

Shape lower edge: Cast on 5 stitches each side every other row for a total of 2 times–68 (72, 76, 80) stitches, ending after a wrong side row.

Work in 10 rows total with olive.

Change to earthtone.

Shape sides: Decrease 1 stitch each side every 18 rows for a

total of 6 times–56 (60, 64, 68) stitches remain.

Work even until piece measures 21 (22, 23, 24)" from beginning, ending after a wrong side row.

Change to olive; work even until piece measures 23 (24, 25, 26)" from beginning.

Bind off remaining stitches loosely, leaving a 4"–5" tail.

## BELT LOOPS (MAKE 6)

Using earthtone, cast on 12 stitches.

Work in Garter stitch (knit every row) for 4 rows.

Bind off all stitches.

## BELT

Using the crochet hook and 2 strands of earthtone held together, chain 225; fasten off.

(Alternatively, braid the belt by using 3 strands of yarn.)

## Finishing:

Weave in ends.

Place Front and Back pieces together, with right sides facing each other and side seams aligned.

Using tapestry needle and the olive tail, sew the olive section together, from top edge along 1 side, to beginning of earthtone section. Using earthtone, continue sewing seam to olive section at lower edge. Using olive tail, sew remainder of seam.

Repeat for other side seam.

Turn skirt right side out.

Belt loops: Place 2 loops approximately 2¹/4" from center Front (4 1/2" apart), even with top edge; using tapestry needle and matching yarn, stitch in place.

Repeat for 2 Back loops, then attach 1 loop at each side seam.

Fringe: Cut 104 strands of earthtone, each 12" long. Divide into 26 groups, 4 strands in each group.

Fold each group in half; using the crochet hook, beginning at side seam on lower edge, pull one group through, form a loop, pull ends through the loop. Attach 13 fringes each to Back and Front, spacing approximately 1" apart.

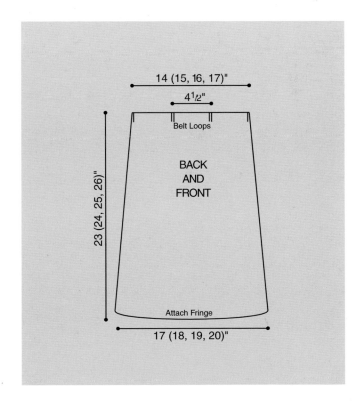

LEFT: *My daughter Hanna is only fourteen, but she looks all grown up in the Bohemian Skirt.*

(CHAPTER 3)
# knitting together

ONE OF THE MANY THINGS I LOVE about knitting is its versatility. You can knit on your own whenever you want some solitude, but you can turn knitting into a social activity too. The potential for social knitting is endless once you start thinking about taking knitting classes, joining or starting a knitting circle, and hosting or attending knitting-themed events.

Whether it's a class or a circle of friends, a knitting group sometimes offers even more than a chance to chat. I'll never forget a woman in my Saturday morning beginner's class. She had been engaged to be married and when the wedding was two months away, her fiancé backed out. Mortified, red-eyed, and miserable, she came to class anyway. Three hours later, after delicious food, affectionate support, and learning something new, she felt much better about herself—so much better, in fact, that she had a different perspective and was almost relieved that her boyfriend had been honest about his feelings before the wedding rather than after. There's a nice communal feeling in a knitting group that makes everyone positive and ready to share and engage with each other. It's very therapeutic.

Classes are probably the best way for beginners to start a knitting social life. You don't have to do anything other than get to class, so all your energy and attention can be poured into learning the basics. Also, when you've paid for something, there's a better chance you'll keep showing up. In my own classes I've seen that eventually students want to branch out. They no longer need my help and they don't feel it's necessary to keep paying for an opportunity to knit. They've got enough motivation on their own. That's how and when a knitting group is born.

## The Knitting Circle

If you can't find an opening in an existing group, a knitting circle is simple and easy to form from scratch. It's very similar to starting a book club—all you need are a few basic ideas to begin. Here are my best suggestions, based on groups I've begun and what I've seen other knitters do.

## Who to Invite

Who you invite to join a knitting circle depends on what you're hoping to get out of it in the first place. If you want a great reason to hang out on a regular basis with the good friends you already have, invite them. If you want to expand your knitting knowledge, ask around at yarn shops to see if more advanced knitters might be interested in joining a group. If you want to start a knitting circle devoted to making warm items to send to war-torn or poverty-stricken areas, look into a religious or civic group for potential members.

What's a good number for a knitting group? That's up to you, and the size of your place. I know circles with four knitters, and others that have eight. In the beginning, I suggest you invite at least twice as many knitters as you think would make an ideal-size group. A few of them won't make it to the first meeting and then there are sure to be dropouts along the way. Begin with a core group of people you know and who are likely candidates for a club. You can then ask each of them to ask one other friend. I think it's better to have too many than too few!

## Finding a Place

Besides someone's house, consider libraries, schools, recreation centers, the Y, churches, bookstores, and knit shops. Think outside the knitting bag. How about the office at lunchtime? A local coffee house? You can sit outside in the park, or even at the beach, in the summer. Why not get a tan at the same time as you knit? (Just keep your knitting out of the sand—and avoid "hairy" yarn that is likely to get sand stuck in it; try linen, cotton, and rayon yarn when at the ocean.) For more ideas, see "On the Move" at right.

## Getting Started

Set a meeting date and then send out printed, flyer-like invitations with logistical information such as time, place, frequency, and what to bring. Or, if you want to be more casual, use the telephone or mention it to people as you bump into them, saying, "Come on over to knit Sunday."

Show-and-tell is a great way to start the first gathering and break the ice. Ask everyone to bring something to share, whether it's a finished piece, a project in progress, or an idea for a project. At the first gathering you can set a regular meeting time. If you agree to meet once a month, for example, then earmark the first Tuesday (or whatever day works best) as a designated meeting date. Often there will be one day of the week that is better for everyone. I think once a month is about the average timing for most knitting circles. If you're all single and don't work ridiculously long hours, maybe you'll want to make it a weekly or biweekly event.

## Keep it Going

One trick to keeping a knitting circle going strong is constantly introducing enticing new projects. Try taking turns suggesting patterns for different meetings. Another way to vary routine is a yarn swap. We did this in one of the

## on the move

Knitting circle meetings can always take place in members' living rooms, but why confine yourselves to the home hearth? Consider changing venues to any of the following kinds of locations, or come up with innovative ideas of your own. Ask permission if your group is more than four or five and especially if the location is small or there's a noise concern.

- Common or public room in a local hotel, resort, bed-and-breakfast, or ski lodge
- Coffeehouse
- Café or boulangerie (during off-peak hours)
- Office building lunchroom or cafeteria
- Bookstore
- Park
- Playground
- Movie theater (catch up on any news or tittle-tattle at next month's meeting)
- Magazine or reading room in the public library (again, you won't be able to chat, but if you all dip into something good at the library, perhaps you'll be inspired to turn your next meeting into a knitting/book discussion combo)
- Recreation center
- Church basement
- Commuter train (knit on the way into the city for a field trip to an exclusive yarn store)
- Baseball game or other sporting event, with or without your spouses

ABOVE: *A knitting party is a great way to build community, exchange ideas, and talk about life.*

knitting groups at my store, and it was very successful. Another idea is to continue with show-and-tell: Have each person bring in a pattern, yarn, or knitting accessory they particularly love and talk about it. Or share a new knitting magazine or book. Having a goal such as knitting for a good cause is a foolproof way to solidify knitting circles. Adopt a group project such as knitting caps for premature babies in the hospital or raising funds for your children's school.

## Knitting Events

By using your imagination, you can introduce a knitting theme to almost any event. From fundraisers and family reunions to cocktail parties and children's birthdays, knitting gives a gathering a festive, focused quality. Knitting also makes for a very relaxed atmosphere, especially good for bringing together guests who don't know each other. In fact, a knitting party would make a great singles event!

The best party I ever gave was my All Girls Night. In Los Angeles, believe it or not, people rarely throw parties because they're so busy. But when I invited fifty of my girlfriends for this unique event, nearly every one of them turned up!

Sometimes girls just want to get together and eat great food without having to think. So I made a huge platter of my favorite entrée, shrimp in a creamy curry, along with a Caesar salad, brown rice, and chocolate-covered strawberries. I served lingonberry martinis, and everybody started knitting, trading ideas, talking, and catching up. Then I had a massage therapist come in and give upper body massages in a back bedroom. We were all in heaven!

Feeling inspired yet? Consider the following elements to create your own knit extravaganza.

## Occasion/Theme

Although you can hold a knitting party for no reason at all, it's also fun to attach a theme or occasion. There's scarcely a week that goes by that doesn't offer some reason for a knitting party. Besides the usual holidays and milestones like Christmas, Valentine's Day, anniversaries, baby showers, and weddings, think spring equinox, first day of school, or National Tree Lovers Day for an excuse to gather friends and celebrate.

## Time/Season

You need enough time to set up, knit for awhile, and still be able to mingle, eat, and drink. Plan on three hours for a knitting event. The time of day and the time of year will be determined by the theme or occasion. Brunch seems just right for baby and wedding showers whereas the evening feels like the right time for a getaway vacation party. Christmas gift-making clearly is in the fall, and birthdays need to be when the guest of honor was born.

## Projects

No one wants to have to concentrate too hard at a party, so simpler projects are usually best for party knitting. Scarves, blankets, cell phone covers, ponchos, and little hats, for example, make good knit activities when you're supplying the patterns. If your pals are already seasoned knitters, you can suggest they bring along whatever they're working on at the moment or request that they knit something for somebody else, like a sweater for a baby.

## Food

When I'm planning a party, I really try to match up the

social occasion with just the right foods. It's a big part of my life. I cook because I love to create and build a story around meals from beginning to end, with the wine, the cheeses, the appetizers, the main course, and desserts.

I tend toward mostly finger foods and put together my favorite dishes that I make over and over. I have lived in several different places and always take what I love, combining Swedish recipes with Tex-Mex and Asian dishes. Another aspect of my cooking style began after I discovered I had an allergy to gluten, which is found in regular wheat flour. Over the years I've learned how to substitute spelt flour, buckwheat flour, brown rice flour, potato flour, and cornmeal, which makes such a difference in the final product. Food seems much lighter without gluten.

I also like food to look pretty. I spend a lot of time thinking about the colors of different foods and how I am going to display them on serving platters. It's all about experimenting and having fun. So use the recipes included here, mix them up with your own, and bon appetit!

## Music

I think the music, along with the food, is the most important ingredient in the recipe for a successful party. Again, I try to carefully choose music that fits the theme or sets just the right tone. It might be cool jazz for a hot summer night, sweet and light Mozart for a mother-daughter tea, or traditional Christmas orchestrations during the holidays. These days it's easy to find a CD with enough selections to keep the party humming for hours.

## Witty, Knitty Invitations

Knitting get-togethers deserve invitations made with all the flair of your best knitting pieces. Try any of the following when planning your next knitting-circle party. Send homemade birthday or greeting cards using these same knit-inspired ideas. Some are more elaborate than others.

**YARN SEWN EDGE:** Choose a pretty handmade paper in an earthy color. Fold in half to make a card. Punch two holes, approximately 2 inches apart, on the folded edge of the card. Leaving one end of yarn outside the holes long enough to tie a bow, weave yarn through the holes to achieve a thick loop of yarn on the card edge. Tie the two ends in a nice bow on either the front or back of the card.

**YARN WRAP:** Squirt craft glue on cardstock, then swirl yarn in a circular pattern or loop up and down and back and forth, completely covering the front of the card. Use a rainbow-colored yarn for a wonderful effect. I've also made cards with yarn glued to the inside in a big swath.

**SWATCH FRONT:** Take a swatch and cut it with sharp scissors or a craft knife in any shape you want: a square, heart, or even a little sweater shape. Let it fray around the edges. Then with a thin thread and needle make a small stitch all the way around, sewing the swatch onto the front of the card. The paper needs to be heavy enough to take the stitch, of course.

Alternatively, cut a sweater, skirt, or dress shape out of the swatch. Glue the shape onto a piece of brown craft paper. Then glue a second, slightly larger piece of cardstock onto the back of the craft paper. Now you have a one-sided card. Nothing cuter. You can sew the swatch on, but glue works fine as long as you use the second sheet of paper for backing.

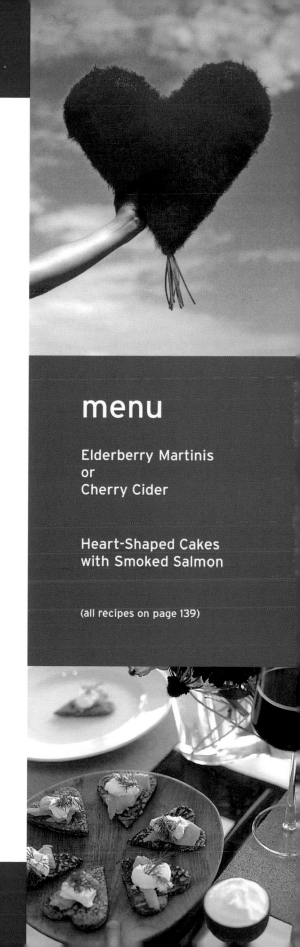

(A KNIT AFFAIR)

# valentine's day

### Occasion/Theme
Midwinter and it's cold outside, but hearts are warmed by a Valentine-inspired knitting event.

### Time/Season
First two weeks in February.

### Project
Valentine Pillow (see page 86). Cupid never had it so good.

### Music
*Love Songs*, Nat King Cole. *The 50 Greatest Love Songs*, Elvis Presley. *Greatest Love Songs*, Frank Sinatra. *Love Songs Collection*, Al Green.

### Variations
Knit the Long Men's Scarf (page 20) for your guy or the Red Riding Hood Scarf (page 53) for your gal.

## menu

**Elderberry Martinis
or
Cherry Cider**

**Heart-Shaped Cakes
with Smoked Salmon**

(all recipes on page 139)

# classic baby set
## with rubber ducky

AT A TRADE SHOW IN ITALY a while ago, I was impressed by the adorable baby clothes, both classic and cute. I came home and created a rayon chenille version of this three-piece set. But chenille can be tricky for handknitting so I switched to cotton yarn for this book. Choose any color you like for the crocheted trim—classic pink or blue for traditionalists or something less conservative for others.

**Experience Level:** Step Up and Knit

**Size:** 3-6 months

**Finished Measurements:**

Cardigan: Chest: 18"; Length 9$1/2$"

Pants: Waist: 18$1/2$"; Length: 13"

Hat: 7" long x 12" circumference

**Materials:**

3 skeins Suss Cotton (100% cotton; 4 ounces/114 grams; 170 yards/156 meters each), color cream

LEFT: *Modify this outfit by sewing on other types of animal appliqués, such as teddy bears or butterflies.*

1 skein Suss Cotton (100% cotton; 4 ounces/114 grams; 170 yards/156 meters each), color baby pink

1 pair size 9 (5.5mm) needles, or size to obtain gauge

1 size G/6 (4mm) crochet hook

Tapestry needle

Sewing needle

Sewing thread

Six wooden buttons–7/8" in diameter

3 rubber duck appliqués (available at fabric stores)

**Gauge:**

16 stitches and 20 rows = 4"/10 cm in Stockinette stitch

**How to Knit:**

### CARDIGAN (BACK)

Using cream, cast on 38 stitches.

Begin Stockinette stitch (knit one right side row and purl one wrong side row).

Work even until piece measures 5$1/4$" from beginning; place a marker each side for armhole.

Continue as established until piece measures 9$1/2$" from the beginning.

Bind off all stitches, placing a marker each side of center 20 stitches for neck. (There are 9 stitches each side for shoulders.)

### CARDIGAN (LEFT FRONT)

Using cream, cast on 28 stitches.

Begin Stockinette stitch.

Work even until piece measures 5$1/4$" from the beginning; place a marker at the beginning of right side row for armhole.

Continue as established until piece measures 8" from the beginning, ending after a right side row.

Shape neck: At neck edge, bind off 19 stitches once–9 stitches remain for shoulder.

Work 7 rows even.

Bind off all stitches.

## CARDIGAN (RIGHT FRONT)

Using cream, cast on 28 stitches.

Begin Stockinette stitch.

Work even until piece measures 2" from the beginning, ending after a wrong side row.

At center Front edge, work 2-row buttonholes this row, then every $2^1/2$" (12 rows) twice more as follows:

Row 1: Knit 3, bind off 2 stitches, knit 8, bind off 2 stitches, work to end.

Row 2: Purl across to first bound off stitches, cast on 2 stitches, purl 8, cast on 2 stitches, work to end. WHILE AT THE SAME TIME, when piece measures $5^1/4$" from the beginning, place a marker at the end of right side row for armhole.

Work even until piece measures same as left Front to neck shaping, ending after a wrong side row.

Continue as for left Front, reversing shaping.

## SLEEVE PANELS (MAKE 4)

Using cream, cast on 14 stitches.

Work even in Stockinette stitch until piece measures 9" from beginning.

Bind off all stitches.

## Finishing:

Weave in ends.

Place right Front on top of Back, wrong sides facing each other.

Using the crochet hook and baby pink, join side seam with single crochet, from lower edge to armhole marker. Join shoulder seam as for side seam.

Repeat for left Front.

Using the crochet hook and baby pink, single-crochet two sleeve pieces together; work 1 row of single crochet around lower edge of sleeve.

Join sleeve to body between markers using single crochet.

Repeat for other sleeve. Roll sleeves up 2" for cuff.

Using the crochet hook and baby pink, single crochet around all edges, beginning in the lower left corner; work up left Front, around neckline, down right Front, and along lower edge. (Note: Work 3 stitches into the same stitch in each corner to round off nicely.)

Align Fronts evenly and mark left Front for button placement. Using sewing needle and thread, attach 6 buttons to left Front.

## PANTS (LEFT LEG)

Using cream, cast on 40 stitches.

Begin Stockinette stitch.

Work even until piece measures $7^1/2$" from the beginning, ending after a right side row.

Shape crotch: Bind off 3 stitches, work to end–37 stitches remain. Work even until piece measures 13" from beginning, ending after a right side row.

Shape waist: At crotch edge, bind off 8 stitches at the beginning of the row every other row twice–21 stitches remain.

Bind off remaining stitches.

## PANTS (RIGHT LEG)

Work as for left leg, reversing all shaping.

## TIE

Using the crochet hook and baby pink, work a chain 36" long for tie.

## Finishing:

Weave in ends.

Fold the left leg in half with right side facing out (bound-off notch should be facing toward you.)

Using the crochet hook and baby pink, join the leg seam with single crochet, beginning at crotch and working to lower edge; do not fasten off. Continuing in single crochet, work around lower edge; fasten off.

Repeat for right leg.

Pin left Front to right Front; pin around to the Back; pin center Back seam. Using the crochet hook and baby pink, join seam with single crochet, beginning at top Front edge, working around to the Back, and ending at Back top edge.

Casing and tie: Fold 1/2" at top edge of pants to inside; pin in place. Using sewing needle and thread, stitch in place, forming a casing for the tie. Using the tapestry needle, thread the tie through and enter into the casing approximately 1/2" from the center Front. Thread the tie through casing, exiting 1/2" from center Front on opposite side.

Position a duck appliqué on each leg, near the lower edge, and sew into place (see photo).

## HAT

### (FRONT AND BACK, BOTH ALIKE)

Using cream, cast on 24 stitches.

Begin Stockinette stitch.

Work even until piece measures 9 1/4" (46 rows) from the beginning; bind off all stitches.

### Finishing:

Weave in ends.

Place the two hat pieces together, with the right side facing out.

Using the crochet hook and baby pink, join the seam with single crochet, beginning at one longer side, working across the top and down the remaining side; do not fasten off. Work 1 row of single crochet around the lower edge of the hat.

Fold the lower edge up 2" for cuff.

Position the third duck appliqué on center Front, or where desired, and stitch in place.

Cut 34 10"-lengths of baby pink yarn. Divide into 2 groups of 17 strands. Fold one group in half. Using a crochet hook, pull the fold through the upper corner of hat to form loop. Pull ends though loop. Repeat on remaining corner.

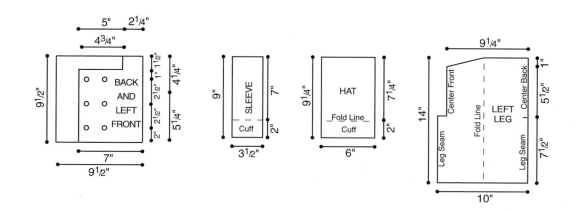

# i'm so
## fuzzy booties

IMAGINE THESE PEEKING OUT of the stroller! Yummy! It's the Voilà yarn that makes them look fuzzy, although I have to admit the yarn is not the easiest to knit with because you can hardly see the stitches through the fuzz. But the result is incredible. My mom made a pair of booties just like these for me when I was a baby.

**Experience Level:** Step Up and Knit

**Size:** 6 months

**Finished Measurements:**

Rib: 2$^{1}/_{2}$" long (folded) by 2$^{1}/_{2}$" wide

Bottom: 5" long (sole) by 1$^{1}/_{2}$" wide

**Materials:**

1 skein Trendsetter Voilà (100% nylon; 1.75 ounces/ 50 grams; 187 yards/172 meters), color mauve

1 skein Suss Ull (100% wool; 2 ounces/57 grams; 215 yards/198 meters each), color pink

1 pair size 7 (4.5mm) needles, or size to obtain gauge

2 small stitch holders

Tapestry needle

**Gauge:** 28 stitches and 32 rows = 4"/10 cm in Stockinette stitch

**How to Knit:**

Divide Suss Ull into two equal-sized balls. Do the same with Voilà.

Using a double strand of Suss Ull, cast on 36 stitches.

Begin 1x1 Rib as follows:

Row 1: *Knit 1, purl 1; repeat from * across.

Row 2: Knit the knit stitches and purl the purl stitches as they face you.

Repeat Rows 1 and 2 for 1x1 Rib.

Work even for 40 rows, ending after a wrong side row.

Dividing row: Place the first and last 12 stitches on a holder for sides.

*LEFT: Wouldn't you love to lounge around and knit while wearing a pair of these booties? I'll have to make a grown-up pattern for them soon.*

Instep and Sole: Join a double strand of Voilà; working on the center 12 stitches only, begin Stockinette stitch (knit one right side row and purl one wrong side row); work even until piece measures 8" from dividing row.

Bind off all stitches. Place a marker 2$^{1}/_{2}$" from Rib section along both sides of Instep and Sole.

Right-hand Side: With right side facing, join a double strand of Voilà; place the first 12 stitches from holder onto the needle, knit 12, then pick up and knit 20 stitches along side of Instep and Sole between Rib section and marker–32 stitches.

Work in Stockinette stitch for 2".

Bind off all stitches.

Left-hand Side: Work as for Right-hand side, beginning at marker on Instep and Sole.

**Finishing:**

Weave in ends.

Fold Instep and Sole section towards sides, with right sides facing each other; line up points X and Y as shown on the diagram.

Using the tapestry needle and Voilà yarn, sew side seams.

Using the tapestry needle and Suss Ull, sew the back seam of the Rib section together. Fold the Rib section in half to form a cuff.

Knit a second bootie to go with the first.

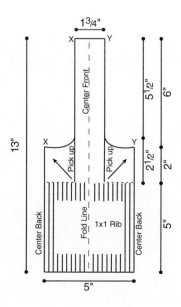

# funky
## purse

THIS PURSE MAKES a great gift for a friend. Whip it up in no time using thick wool on big needles. Its small bamboo handle and lining in contrasting color make it unique. A crocheted wool and chocolate-leather bloom gives it flower power.

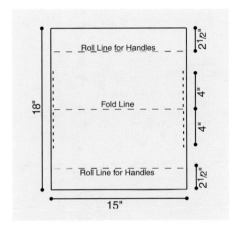

**Experience Level:** Cinchy for Starters

**Knitted Measurements:**

15" wide x 18" long

**Finished Measurements:**

14" x 7" (after ring handles attached)

**Materials:**

1 skein Brown Sheep Company's Burly Spun (100% wool; 8 oz/ 228 grams; 132 yards/121 meters each), color #110 orange

*LEFT: Vary this design by substituting a leather or crocheted strap for the bamboo handles.*

1 pair size 15 (10mm) needles, or size to obtain gauge

Tapestry needle

Sewing needle and thread

15" x 17" lining fabric (vintage silk, denim, or other lining material)

*1 pair tortoise shell or bamboo circular rings, each 1" thick and 6" in diameter (for handles)

*One leather flower

*Available at Suss Design, see page 134

**Gauge:**

8 stitches and 12 rows = 4"/10 cm in Stockinette stitch

**How to knit:**

Cast on 30 stitches.

Work even in Stockinette stitch (knit one right side row and purl one wrong side row) until piece measures 18" from the beginning.

Bind off all stitches.

**Finishing:**

Weave in ends.

Side seams: Fold knitted piece in half and hold together with right sides facing each other; using sewing needle and thread, seam piece 4 " up from fold on each side (see diagram). Turn piece right-side out.

Attach handles: Roll 2½" of the cast-on edge tightly around one of the ring handles; whipstitch in place. Roll 2½" of bind-off edge tightly around the other ring handle; whipstitch in place.

Lining: Fold lining fabric in half and hold together with right sides facing each other. Seam piece 4" up from fold on each side; do not turn right-side out.

Place lining inside purse and sew into place, covering seams where handles were attached; allow fabric to gather along ring handles as necessary.

# hooded
## flag pullover

EVERY SUMMER MY FAMILY JOINS a group of other families at the Hollywood Bowl to celebrate the Fourth of July. We get dressed up in patriotic colors for the all-out occasion, complete with fireworks, a picnic dinner, and champagne. Often the night gets chilly, so I made this sweater for all the kids to keep them warm as they fall asleep in their parents' arms. The hood makes it perfect for weekends, and the vintage colors make it a bit more sophisticated than the typical child's garment.

*LEFT: Dana Reber was celebrating her birthday the day we photographed her in this pullover, her birthday present from me.*

**Experience Level:** Hot Knitters

**Sizes:** 2 (4, 6) years

**Finished Measurements:**

Chest: 28 (30, 32)"

Length: 14 (15, 17)"

**Materials:**

3 (3, 4) skeins Suss Cotton (100% cotton; 4 ounces/ 114 grams; 170 yards/156 meters each), color naturale,

1 skein Suss Cotton (100% cotton; 4 ounces/114 grams; 170 yards/156 meters each), color poppy

1 skein Suss Cotton (100% cotton; 4 ounces/114 grams; 170 yards/156 meters each), color mood indigo

1 pair size 8 (5mm) needles, or size to obtain gauge

Tapestry needle

Stitch holder

**Gauge:** 16 stitches and 24 rows = 4"/10 cm in Stockinette stitch

**How to Knit:**

### BACK

Using naturale, cast on 56 (60, 64) stitches.

Begin Stockinette stitch (knit one right side row and purl one wrong side row); work even until piece measures 13½ (14½, 16)" [80 (86, 96) rows] from the beginning, ending after a wrong side row.

Shape shoulders: Bind off 8 (8, 6) stitches each side 2 (2, 3) times–24 (28, 28) stitches remain.

Bind off remaining stitches.

## FRONT

Using naturale, cast on 56 (60, 64) stitches.

Begin Stockinette stitch; work even in Stripe sequence as follows:

12 rows naturale

12 rows poppy

Continue in Stripe sequence, alternating 12 rows of each color, until piece measures 8 (8½, 10)" from the beginning [48 (54, 60) rows], ending after a wrong side row. (Note: For size 4, flag begins in the center of a naturale stripe.)

Establish Intarsia (Flag): Continuing in Stripe sequence, knit 28 (30, 32); join mood indigo, work to end. (Note: To avoid holes between the colors—twist strands together at each color change on the wrong side of work; be sure that the yarn you start working with comes on top.)

Continuing as established, work even until piece measures 10½ (11¼, 13¼)" [63 (67, 79) rows] from the beginning, ending after a right side row; place a marker each side of center 14 (18, 18) stitches.

Shape neck: Work across to marker; bind off the center stitches; work to end—21 (21, 23) stitches remaining each shoulder. Place the right shoulder stitches on a holder to be worked on later.

Left neck and shoulder: Working on the left shoulder stitches only,

Shape neck: Continuing as established, at neck edge (end of right side rows), decrease 1 stitch every other row 5 times—16 (16, 18) stitches remain for shoulder; work even until piece measures same as Back to Shoulder shaping, ending after a wrong side row.

Shape shoulder: At armhole edge, bind off 8 (8, 6) stitches every other row 2 (2, 3) times.

Right neck and shoulder: Work as for left neck and shoulder, reversing shaping.

## SLEEVES
## (MAKE 1 NATURALE AND 1 POPPY)

Using naturale, cast on 28 (28, 30) stitches.

Begin Stockinette stitch.

Shape sleeve: Increase 1 stitch each side every 8 (7, 7) rows for a total of 7 (9, 10) times—42 (46, 50) stitches. Work even until piece measures 10 (11, 12)" from the beginning.

Bind off all stitches.

Make second sleeve same as the first, but work in poppy.

## HOOD

Using naturale, cast on 5 (6, 6) stitches.

Begin Stockinette stitch; work even for 2 rows, ending after a wrong side row.

Shape neck edge: Cast on 5 (6, 6) stitches at the beginning of this row, then every other row a total of 4 (4, 5) times—25 (30, 36) stitches.

Cast on 7 (4, 0) stitches every other row once—32 (34, 36) stitches.

Work even until piece measures 10 ¾ (11¼, 11¾)" from the beginning, measured along longer edge, ending after a wrong side row.

Shape center Back: Decrease 1 stitch every other row 5 times, ending after a wrong side row.

Increase 1 stitch every other row 5 times (to create a V-shaped notch—see diagram).

Work even until piece measures 22½ (23½, 24½)" from the beginning, ending after a wrong side row.

Shape neck edge: Bind off 7 (4, 0) stitches at the beginning of this row, then 5 (6, 6) stitches every other row 4 (4, 5) times—5 (6, 6) stitches remain.

Bind off remaining stitches.

## Finishing:

Weave in ends.

Stars: Randomly embroider stars on flag section of Front, approximately 1" in diameter, as follows:

Thread tapestry needle with naturale yarn. Make a 5-point star by connecting the points with the yarn (see diagram).

Place Front and Back pieces together with right sides facing each other. Using the tapestry needle and yarn, sew shoulder seams. Measure up from lower edge 8 (8½, 10)"; place a marker for beginning of armhole. Sew side seam, beginning at lower edge, ending at armhole marker.

Fold sleeves lengthwise and sew sleeve seam. Pin, then sew sleeves between markers, sewing the poppy sleeve onto side with Flag.

Hood: Fold piece in half, with right sides facing each other. Sew the shorter side, including the notch, together.

Place a marker at center Back neck of sweater; placing hood seam at center marker, sew the hood evenly to neck shaping.

**HOOD**

Neck Edge — 2"

8³/₄ (9¹/₄, 9³/₄)"

24¹/₂ (25¹/₂, 26¹/₂)"

Fold Line — 3"

Center Back Seam Line

8³/₄ (9¹/₄, 9³/₄)"

Seam Line

Neck Edge — 2"

8 (8¹/₂, 9)"

---

4 (4, 4¹/₂)"

6 (7, 7)"

1/2"

Naturale

Poppy

3¹/₂ (3³/₄, 3³/₄)"

Mood Indigo

Naturale

BACK

Poppy

AND

Naturale

FRONT

Poppy

Naturale

14 (15, 17)"

5¹/₂ (6, 6¹/₂)"

8 (8¹/₂, 10)"

14 (15, 16)"

---

10¹/₂ (11¹/₂, 12¹/₂)"

**SLEEVE**

10 (11, 12)"

7 (7, 7¹/₂)"

---

5-Pointed Star

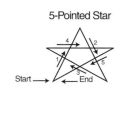

Start → ← End

# valentine
## pillow

**NOBODY CAN RESIST** this heart pillow, and, of course, it lasts forever instead of fading like Valentine roses. You knit two pieces, hand-stitch them together, and stuff with something soft, maybe even some freshly dried lavender for a sensuous scent. The yarn is the softest red/pink Suss Fuzzy—my most popular yarn combo. You could make it in other colors for a beautiful accent in any area you place it.

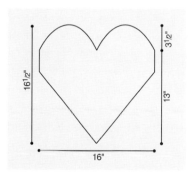

**Experience Level:** Cinchy for Starters

**Final Measurements:** 16½" long x 16" at widest point across

**Materials:** 4 skeins Suss Fuzzy (60% cotton/40% nylon; 2 ounces/57 grams; 67 yards/62 meters each), color red/pink

1 pair size 10 (6mm) needles, or size to obtain gauge

Tapestry needle

1 stitch holder

6 yards of pink leather lacing

Pillow stuffing

*LEFT: You don't have to wear your heart on your sleeve, you can put it on the couch with this pillow.*

**Gauge:** 16 stitches and 20 rows = 4"/10 cm in Stockinette stitch

**How to knit:**

Back and Front (both alike): Cast on 4 stitches.

Begin Stockinette stitch (knit one right side row and purl one wrong side row).

Shape sides: Increase 1 stitch each side every row 4 times, ending after a wrong side row–12 stitches.

Increase 1 stitch each side every other row for a total of 24 times, ending after a wrong side row–60 stitches.

Work even for 16 rows, ending after a wrong side row.

Dividing row: Work across 30 stitches (left top); place remaining 30 stitches on holder (right top). Work 1 row even.

Left top: Decrease 1 stitch each side every other row for a total of 6 times–18 stitches remain.

Decrease 1 stitch on each side every row for a total of 4 times–10 stitches remain.

Bind off remaining stitches.

Right top: Place stitches from holder onto needle; work as for left top.

**Finishing:**

Weave in ends.

Place the Back and Front together, right sides facing each other. Using the tapestry needle threaded with yarn, sew pieces together, leaving approximately 3" open at the lower edge for stuffing; turn pillow right-side out. Stuff pillow evenly. Fold seam edges to the inside and finish sewing the pillow together with a whipstitch on the outside.

Leather edging: Thread the tapestry needle with leather lacing; work whipstitch around the pillow edges.

Tassel: Cut 12 strands of leather lacing, each 10" long. Fold 10 strands in half; using another strand, tie them together at the fold. Wind the last strand several times around top of folded strands, 1 inch down from top.

Conceal the ends and sew the Tassel to the point.

# baby's
# first blanket

A GROUP OF THE NEW parents' friends can make this lovely shower gift together; each person knits one square in the same cotton yarn but in a variety of stitch patterns. Seed stitch, Garter stitch, striped Stockinette stitch, and 2 x 2 Rib stitch make the blanket look plush. The best finisher crochets the individually knit sections together, creating an instant heirloom to pass down for generations.

**Experience Level:** Cinchy for Starters

**Finished Measurements:** 30" square

## Materials:

3 skeins Suss Cotton (100% cotton; 4 ounces/114 grams; 182 yards/167 meters each), color naturale

2 skeins Suss Cotton (100% cotton; 4 ounces/114 grams; 182 yards/167 meters each), color chamoise (yellow)

2 skeins Suss Cotton (100% cotton; 4 ounces/114 grams; 182 yards/167 meters each), color honey

LEFT: *Simply triple or quadruple the number of squares you knit to create a unique throw instead of a baby blanket.*

1 skein Suss Cotton (100% cotton; 4 ounces/114 grams; 182 yards/167 meters each), celery

1 pair size 9 (5.5mm) needles, or size to obtain gauge

1 size G/6 (4mm) crochet hook

## Gauge:

16 stitches and 24 rows = 4"/10 cm in Stockinette stitch

## How to Knit:

### 2 X 2 RIBBED SQUARE (MAKE 2)

Using naturale, cast on 40 stitches.

Begin 2 x 2 Ribbed stitch as follows:

Row 1: *Knit 2, purl 2; repeat from * across.

Row 2: Knit the knit stitches and purl the purl stitches as they face you.

Repeat Rows 1 and 2 for Ribbed stitch.

Work even until piece measures 10" (60 rows) from the beginning.

Bind off all stitches.

### STRIPED SQUARE (MAKE 3)

Using celery, cast on 40 stitches.

Begin Stockinette stitch (knit one right side row and purl one wrong side row); work even for a total of 12 rows.

Change to naturale; work for a total of 12 rows.

Continue to alternate colors every 12 rows until piece measures 10" (60 rows) from the beginning, ending after working 12 rows with celery (3 stripes in celery and 2 stripes in naturale).

Bind off all stitches.

## SEED STITCH SQUARE (MAKE 2)

Using chamoise, cast on 40 stitches.

Begin Seed stitch as follows:

Row 1: *Knit 1, purl 1; repeat from * across.

Row 2: *Purl 1, knit 1; repeat from * across. (Knit the purls and purl the knits as they face you.)

Work even until piece measures 10" (60 rows) from the beginning.

Bind off all stitches.

## GARTER STITCH SQUARE (MAKE 2)

Using honey, cast on 40 stitches.

Begin Garter stitch (knit every row); work even until piece measures 10" (60 rows) from the beginning.

Bind off all stitches.

## Finishing:

Weave in ends.

Block each piece to a uniform 10" square.

Lay out all squares. Place a Striped square in center and 2 at opposite corners; place the Ribbed squares at the other corners; place the Garter stitch squares across from each other and the Seed stitch squares across from each other (see diagram).

(Note: If you prefer, mix them in a more random fashion.)

Using the crochet hook and naturale, single crochet the squares together.

Blanket edging: Beginning at one corner, *work in single crochet to next corner, work space for tassel at corner as follows:

In corner stitch, work (1 single crochet, chain 2, 1 single crochet); repeat from * twice, then continue in single crochet to where you began, single crochet in beginning corner st, chain 2, slip stitch into the beginning single crochet. Fasten off.

Tassels: Cut 80 lengths of naturale, each 20" long.

Divide into 4 groups.

Fold one group in half. Using a crochet hook, pull the group through the chain–2 stitches at the corner of the blanket to form a loop. Pull ends through the loop to complete the tassel.

Repeat on the 3 remaining corners.

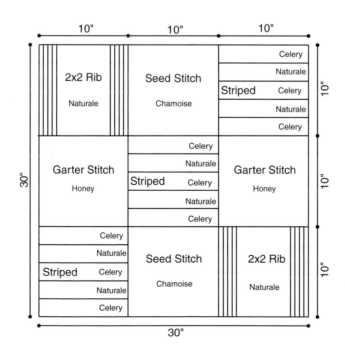

# midsummer
# bikini

I HAVE A PASSION for knitted bikinis—having grown up in the 1970s when they were so popular. Stylish yet easy to knit, this bikini is not practical for swimming, but for sunbathing, yes! The string ties are adjustable on the sides and around the back and neck. You could wear just the top with army pants, or only the bottom and a white tee. I picked colors in my space-dyed cotton that remind me of midsummer eve in Sweden.

**Experience Level:** Step Up and Knit

**Size:** Medium
(To fit women who wear approximately sizes 4–8)

## Finished Measurements:

Bottom: 18" long

Top: 6" long

## Materials:

2 skeins Suss Spacedye (100% cotton; 4 ounces/114 grams; 190 yards/175 meters each), color painted desert

1 pair size 9 (5.5mm) needles, or size to obtain gauge

1 size G/6 (4mm) crochet hook

Sewing needle

Sewing thread

Tapestry needle

## Gauge:

16 stitches and 20 rows = 4"/10 cm in Stockinette stitch

## How to Knit:

### BOTTOM

Cast on 48 stitches.

Begin Stockinette stitch (knit one right side row and purl one wrong side row).

Casing: Work even until piece measures 2" (10 rows) from the beginning, ending after a wrong side row.

Shape leg openings: Decrease 1 stitch each side this row, then every 3 rows for a total of 19 times–10 stitches remain.

Increase 1 stitch each side every 3 rows for a total of 9 times–28 stitches.

Casing: Work even for 10 rows.

Bind off stitches loosely.

## TIES (MAKE 2)

Using a double strand of yarn and crochet hook, work a chain 42" long.

### Finishing:

Weave in ends.

Fold casing to wrong side, 1" from both cast-on and bound-off edges. Pin into place; using a threaded sewing needle, sew casing to inside.

Using the crochet hook, work 1 row of single crochet around leg openings, beginning and ending at casing. (Don't close casing ends.) Using the tapestry needle, thread the ties through the casings of both pieces. Tie an overhand knot at each end of ties to finish.

### LEFT TOP

Cast on 28 stitches.

Begin Stockinette stitch.

Casing: Work even until piece measures 2" (10 rows) from the beginning, ending after a wrong side row.

Shape sides: At armhole edge (beginning of right side rows), decrease 1 stitch every 3 rows for a total of 9 times, WHILE AT THE SAME TIME, at center Front (end of right side rows), decease 1 stitch every row 6 times, then 1 stitch every other row 11 times—2 stitches remaining.

Bind off remaining stitches.

### RIGHT TOP

Work as for left Top, reversing all shaping.

### TIES

Using the crochet hook and a double strand of yarn, work a chain 50" long.

### Finishing:

Weave in ends.

Fold casing to wrong side, 1" from cast-on edge. Pin into place; using a threaded sewing needle, sew casing to inside.

Using the crochet hook, work 1 row of single crochet around armhole and center Front edges. beginning and ending at casing. (Don't close casing ends.) Using the tapestry needle, thread the tie through the casings of both pieces. Tie an overhand knot through each end of tie to finish.

LEFT: *While you can't swim in this bikini, you can shine in it poolside.*

Neck straps: Using the crochet hook and a double strand of yarn, attach yarn at upper point (bound off edge); work a chain 21" long; fasten off.

Repeat for second half of top.

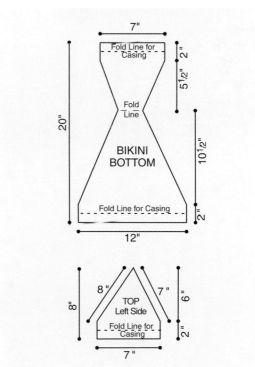

# (CHAPTER 4)
# knitting bag
# of tricks

THIS CHAPTER REALLY IS A GRAB BAG of practical techniques and fun suggestions that can make knitting even more enjoyable.

## Twist and Shout: Making Your Own Yarn

Okay, I don't mean starting from scratch with sheep and a spinning wheel. I mean customizing yarn you buy, usually through mixing. Sometimes I combine as many as ten different skeins of yarn into one ball and knit it with gigantic needles. When you work with your own custom blends, you can be sure that you're making a project unlike anyone else's. Here's my ridiculously easy technique:

- Choose the yarns you'd like to combine. Think about mixing different colors, weights, and textures.
- Wind each of your chosen yarns into a ball.
- Put all the balls in a basket with a handle.
- Find the beginning end of each ball and start knitting.

Of course, you can make one ball out of, say, five different yarns, which is what I do. But keeping each yarn separate in your basket gives you more flexibility—this way you can still use any of the yarns for something else.

## Hang it Up: Decorating with Yarn

For as long as I can remember I've used yarn to add color and style to my surroundings. In New York, I kept yarn in small wooden boxes on industrial metal shelves all over my bedroom. Every morning when I woke up I would think, "Hmmm, what should I knit today?" At my store right now, high above one side of the register I have all pink yarn, and the other side is all black and creams, and then I have all blues hanging over the table where my beginner's classes are held. At the entrance to the store is a mannequin wrapped in plump, super-bulky green yarn. Hanging from a rod near the advanced knitting group couch area are skeins of green yarn in every shade I could find.

Here are some guidelines for getting into the yarn-decorating groove.

Hang hanks of yarn from rods or even real tree branches suspended from the ceiling. Vary the yarn lengths, textures, and styles but keep all the yarn in the same color family for gorgeous effect. Create a small artwork or a whole room divider using this idea.

Next time your yarn gets tangled like spaghetti and you don't want to untangle it, use it for home décor projects. Try piling it in unusual, clear, oversized containers. For the store, I combined a hundred different yarns in four huge beautiful jars. I used leather yarn, wool yarn, metallic yarn, nearly every texture I could find—it took me three hours to fill them! If you layer colors like pink, orange, and red, it looks like a sunset. Using brown, green, and blue creates a landscape effect. Kids love to do this too. Give them smaller jars and see what they create.

Let the containers you already own inspire you. A friend made me a basketweave bowl out of rough clay; I immediately put in a dozen balls of cream yarn. With a few knitting needles strategically placed, it's a simple and elegant still-life on a side table in my living room.

Braid several colors of strong yarn and use it to make a rope for hanging a plant. Or braid more delicate yarn to make napkin rings.

RIGHT: *A few easy ways to decorate your home with yarn.*

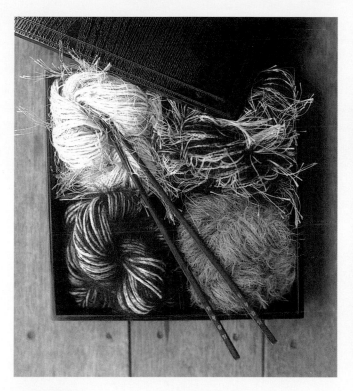

## All the Trimmings

With so many exotic trimming options, it's sometimes hard to narrow down the choices for a project. I use whatever strikes my fancy and suits the weight of the yarn and style of the piece.

### BUTTONS

Buttons are both functional and decorative. Scout for unusual ones year-round and you'll end up with quite a collection. If you're making an autumn wrap or a bag that's not too dainty, choose a big, hand-carved wooden toggle button that echoes the earthiness of the wool.

### BEADS

I use beads quite a lot in my knits. It's easy to buy yarns with sequins already sewn in, and I do that regularly. But I also love to sew oversized individual beads onto bulky sweaters, larger bags, and wraps. Look for big, bold beads with irregular shapes and textures. For more delicate pieces, I like Austrian crystals, which are pretty little glass beads that come in many different sizes. To give a little edge to a winter hat, finish off the fringe or crochet string or loop on the top with five or six beads rather than a tassel or pompom. To sew beads onto a project, use either silk or soft metal threads.

### FUR

I love fake fur for trimming purses, cardigans, and wraps. It's reasonably priced and comes by the yard in different weights and widths in prints and solids at most sewing stores. And a little bit goes a long way. I use a taupe-colored fur for many items because the color goes with everything. One season I put 6-inch wide fur cuffs and a big fur collar on a fitted cardigan.

### LEATHER

Leather makes a handsome, understated trim. I made a long coat with a little fake fur collar and a half-inch-wide hand-cut leather strap trim around the cuffs. You might also mix leather straps with your tassels and pompom yarn.

## Beyond the Basics

### EVALUATING PATTERNS

I always advise knitters to read through patterns start to finish before they even buy the yarn so they are sure they understand what they're going to be doing and believe they're going to enjoy doing it. This helps to avoid wasted time and money. Here are some basic guidelines for evaluating a pattern.

Avoid patterns written with too many abbreviations unless you can easily understand what they all mean. (To avoid confusion, I skip the abbreviations and write everything out in my patterns.) Check out the photo of the project and, if there is one, the schematic (the flat diagram showing the shape of the project) to see if it looks complicated. While my Magic Wrap Vest (page 56) may look complicated in the photo, if you look at the schematic you will see that it's simply two easy pieces sewn together. No matter what else is going on in a pattern, the simpler the shape, the easier it's going to be to knit.

Don't be shy about asking salespeople to give you their opinion on the difficulty of a pattern. It's their job to keep you coming back for more yarn to knit, so they want to help you find patterns that match your skill level.

## AVOIDING KNITTER'S BLOCK

In general, if you quit knitting, you quit. I've known people who get a high-pressure job and stop knitting, for instance. But sometimes I have students who just don't like certain projects. One started making the Serendipity Cardigan from my last book, but she only really liked to make scarves, so she suffered a case of knitter's block. On top of that, she knitted it too tight, she didn't measure her gauge, and she had to take it all out and knit it again. Such a waste of yarn, money, and time.

To avoid knitter's block, here's some advice.

Be sure to only start projects you think you will enjoy knitting. Even if the project is big or a bit hard, if you feel passionate about it, you're likely to finish it. It took one of my students nine months to finish the Fantasy Throw (page 116). Admittedly, she got a little bored, but she stuck with it, and the day she sewed together all the pieces, everyone stood up and applauded. And she felt really good about her accomplishment.

Choose a pattern that matches your skill level. If it's just too hard to knit, of course you will get frustrated and blocked. Although I like to encourage everyone to finish projects, sometimes it's best to put a project aside for awhile.

### keeping extra yarn around

After completing a project, be sure to keep at least ten feet of the yarn as well as any additional accessories, such as spare buttons, in a safe place. You never know when you'll need to make a repair.

Don't work on more than three items at a time or you're bound not to finish some.

If you start feeling bored, take a break. Don't stop knitting, just pick up a quick and easy project. Take a knitting break instead of a coffee break and come back refreshed.

## It's in the Bag

I think in-progress knitting projects deserve pretty containers. So when I saw my customers carrying around their projects in brown paper bags from the store, I decided to design special bags for sale only. They are a very simple, classic knitting bag shape with knitting-needle handles. Their pizzazz comes from the fabric they're sewn out of— either vintage denim, silk dupioni, or fake fur. I also designed a mini, semi-transparent bag out of lavender, gray, and pink chiffon to hold small projects.

Other creative ideas for knitting containers are baskets, plastic totes, fabric-covered cardboard boxes, and old-fashioned red toolboxes. If you're ever in town, stop by the store for one of our special bags made out of natural-colored fake fur. Everyone will know you're a knitter with *livsglädje* as you swing down the street.

## Knitter's Massage

I knit every day for twenty years before realizing how beneficial massage could be, especially for my upper back, shoulders, and hands. Now that I know, I'm hooked. I have regular professional massages at least once a month, and I make a point of massaging my hands with a rich hand cream every night.

The following stretches will improve endurance and flexibility in your wrists, hands and fingers.

### HAND MASSAGE

Place the thumb of your left hand in the palm of your right hand and simultaneously wrap the fingers of your left hand around your right. Massage for one minute. Repeat on the other hand.

### CLENCH AND FAN

Clench one hand into a tight fist and hold it like this for five seconds. Release your hand gradually, extending the thumb and fingers into a fully open position. Hold this for another five seconds. Repeat five times for each hand.

### THUMB STRETCH

Place the thumb of your left hand on top of your right thumb and gently press down with your left thumb so that your right thumb extends toward your right forearm. Hold the stretch for five seconds. You should feel the stretch in the base of the thumb on the palm side. Repeat this for the left hand. Alternate thumbs and repeat five times for each.

### WRIST STRETCH

Hold your right hand straight out in front of you, with the palm facing away from you and your fingers together and pointing up. With your left hand, gently pull the right hand's outstretched fingers toward you. Hold for five seconds. You should feel a stretch in your right wrist. Repeat for the left hand. Repeat five times for each hand, alternating hands.

### WRIST CIRCLES

With your elbows bent comfortably, hold your hands in front of you and gently rotate your wrists. Then, switch directions. Repeat five times in each direction for each hand.

(A KNIT AFFAIR)

# wedding shower
## brunch

### Occasion/Theme
Make something lovely for a friend's once-in-a-lifetime day.

### Time/Season
Any time of year on a Saturday or Sunday, late morning or early afternoon.

### Project
Fantasy Throw (page 116). A honeymooner's delight.

### Music
Upbeat love songs! *Going to the Chapel, I'm in Love with a Wonderful Guy.*

### Variations
Knit the Funky Purse (page 80) for the bride-to-be's trousseau.

## menu

**Bellinis or Fresh Peach Juice Spritzers**

**Delicate Potato Cakes with Shrimp and Eggs**

**Buckwheat Cookies**

(all recipes on page 139)

# zip-up
## pullover

The colors and zippers add a modern touch, yet the shape goes with everything. This sweater was in *Parents* magazine on a new mom, who said it made her feel especially stylish right after having her baby. It's also a great sweater to wear during pregnancy, opening the front zipper as your belly grows.

**Experience Level:** Step Up and Knit

**Sizes:** Extra-Small (Small, Medium, Large)

**Finished Measurements:**

Chest: 28 (30, 32, 34)"

Length: 24 (25, 26, 27)"

**Materials:**

3 (3, 3, 4) skeins Suss Bomull (100% cotton; 4 ounces/114 grams; 190 yards/175 meters each), color olive

2 skeins Suss Bomull (100% cotton; 4 ounces/114 grams; 190 yards/175 meters each), color light blue

1 pair size 10 (6mm) needles, or size to obtain gauge

2 stitch holders

Tapestry needle

Sewing needle

LEFT: *Whenever you wear this sweater, open or close the zippers depending on your mood. I could rename it the Mood Pullover.*

1 zipper (closed end) 8 (8, 9, 9)" long

2 zippers (closed end) 9" long (all sizes)

**Gauge:**

16 stitches and 20 rows = 4"/10 cm in Stockinette stitch

**How to Knit:**

BACK

Using olive, cast on 62 (66, 70, 74) stitches.

Begin Stockinette stitch (knit one right side row and purl one wrong side row).

Shape sides: Decrease 1 stitch each side every 20 rows for a total of 3 times–56 (60, 64, 68) stitches remain.

Work even until piece measures 14 (14$^{1}/_{2}$, 15$^{1}/_{4}$, 15$^{3}/_{4}$)" from the beginning, ending after a wrong side row.

Change to light blue; work even for 10 (10, 12, 12) rows, ending after a wrong side row.

Shape Armholes: Bind off 2 stitches each side once – 52 (56, 60, 64) stitches remain.

Decrease 1 stitch each side every other row for a total of 1 (1, 2, 2) times–50 (54, 56, 60) stitches remain.

Work even until armhole measures 7 (7 $^{1}/_{2}$, 7 $^{1}/_{2}$, 8)" from the beginning of shaping, ending after a wrong side row; place a marker each side of center 10 (14, 14, 16) stitches.

Shape shoulders and neck: Work across to marker; place remaining sts on a holder for right shoulder and neck. At neck edge, bind off 10 stitches once, 5 stitches once, WHILE AT THE SAME TIME, at armhole edge, bind off 2 stitches twice, bind off remaining stitches.

Right neck and shoulder: Join yarn at neck, ready to work a right side row; bind off center stitches for neck. Work as for left shoulder, reversing shaping.

## FRONT

Using 2 separate balls of olive, cast on 31 (33, 35, 37) stitches with each ball.

Begin Stockinette stitch.

Working each section at the same time with separate balls, work as for Back, shaping sides, until piece measures 8 (8, 9, 9.)" Join pieces and work until Front measures 12 (13, 14, 15)" from the beginning, ending after a wrong side row.

Change to light blue yarn and work as for Back for remainder of piece.

## SLEEVES (MAKE 2)

Using olive, cast on 50 (54, 54, 56) stitches.

Begin Stockinette stitch.

Shape sleeves: Decrease 1 stitch each side every 28 (32, 40, 44) rows for a total of 3 (3, 2, 2) times–44 (48, 50, 52) stitches remain.

WHILE AT SAME TIME, when piece measures 17 (18, 18 3/4, 18 3/4)" from the beginning, change to light blue; work 10 (10, 12, 12) rows, completing shaping–piece measures 19 (20, 21, 21)" from beginning.

10 (11, 11,

BACK
AND
FRON

24 (25, 26, 27)"

Insert Zipper (front only)

14 (15,

15 1/2 (16 1/2, 1

Repeat Rows 1 and 2 for 1 x 1 Rib.

Work 6 rows even.

Change to larger needles and Stockinette stitch (knit one right side row and purl one wrong side row). Work even until piece measures 10 (11, 11 1/2, 12)" from the beginning, ending after a wrong side row.

Edging: Change to smaller needles and 1 x 1 Rib; work 6 rows even.

Bind off all stitches.

## FRONT

Work as for Back until piece measures 10 (11, 11 1/2, 12)" from the beginning.

Continuing in Stockinette stitch, work until piece measures same as Back to bind off, ending after a wrong side row–11 (12, 12 1/2, 13)" from the beginning.

Shape armholes: Bind off 3 stitches on each side once, then decrease 1 stitch on each side every 3 rows for a total of 6 (6, 8, 8) times–34 (38, 38, 42) stitches remain.

Decrease 1 stitch each side every other row for a total of 7 (8, 7, 8) times, WHILE AT THE SAME TIME, when piece measures 16 (16 1/2, 17 1/4, 18)" from the beginning, end after a wrong side row; place a marker each side of center 10 (12, 12, 14) stitches.

Shape left neck: Work across to marker (left Front); place remaining stitches on holder (neck and right Front). At neck edge, bind off 5 (5, 6, 6) stitches once.

Shape right neck: Join yarn at neck edge, ready to work a right side row on stitches on holder. Bind off center 10 (12, 12, 14) stitches, work to end. Complete as for left neck.

## STRAPS (MAKE 2)

Using smaller needles, cast on 7 stitches; work in 1 x 1 Rib until piece measures 28" from the beginning.

Bind off all stitches.

## CROCHET STRINGS (MAKE 2)

Using the crochet hook, work a chain 28" long.

## Finishing:

Weave in ends.

Attach ring: Wrap the top edge of Front piece around the ring, gathering inside ring; pin in place. Using the tapestry needle and yarn, stitch edge neatly to inside, stretching as needed.

Attach straps: At the top of ring, wrap one end of each strap around the ring; pin, then sew it into place.

Lay Back piece on top of Front piece with right sides facing each other. Sew side seams together. Sew the crochet strings into each side seam, approximately 1/2" down from bound off edge of the Back piece.

Turn piece right-side out.

Using the crochet hook or tapestry needle, bring each crochet string to the right side of the Back. Weave each string in and out through the 1 x 1 Rib at the top of piece, towards center Back, approximately 1" apart, until they meet.

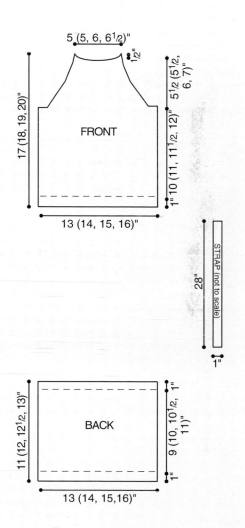

LEFT: Actress Lisa Edelstein began taking my knitting classes years ago. She is becoming a great knitter.

marker each side of center 16 stitches.

Shape left shoulder and neck: At armhole edge, bind off 10 (10, 11, 12) stitches, work to marker; place center 16 stitches on a stitch holder for neck; place remaining stitches on a stitch holder for left shoulder. Working on right shoulder stitches only, work 1 row even.

At neck edge, bind off 6 (6, 7, 8) stitches once, WHILE AT THE SAME TIME, at armhole edge, bind off 10 (11, 11, 11) stitches every other row twice.

Right shoulder and neck: Work as for left shoulder, reversing all shaping.

### FRONT

Work as for Back until piece measures 24½ (25½, 26½, 27½)" from the beginning, ending after a wrong side row; place a marker each side of center 20 (20, 22, 24) stitches.

Shape neck: Work across to marker; place the center 20 (20, 22, 24) stitches on a stitch holder for neck; place remaining stitches on a stitch holder for right shoulder.

At neck edge, decrease 1 stitch every other row for a total of 4 times, WHILE AT THE SAME TIME, when piece measures same as Back to shoulder shaping, end after a wrong side row.

Shape shoulder as for Back.

Right shoulder: Work as for left shoulder, reversing all shaping.

### SLEEVES (MAKE 2)

Using a double strand of ash, cast on 38 (40, 42, 44) stitches.

Begin Stockinette stitch; work in Stripe Sequence as for Back for entire piece.

Shape sleeves: Increase 1 stitch on each side every 7 (7, 7, 6) rows for a total of 13 (14, 15, 16) times—64 (68, 72, 76) stitches. Work even until piece measures 20½ (21½, 22½, 22½)" from the beginning.

Bind off all stitches.

### Finishing:

Weave in ends.

Place Front and Back pieces together right sides facing each other. Using the tapestry needle and yarn, sew shoulder seams, matching shaping.

LEFT: *Artist Andre Miripolsky has been wearing my sweaters for years now—as long as I've been admiring his paintings.*

Neck: With right side facing, using circular knitting needle and ash, pick up and knit 60 (60, 64, 68) stitches around neck shaping, including stitches on holders [28 (28, 30, 32) stitches along Back neck, 32 (32, 34, 36) stitches along Front neck]; place a marker for beginning of round.

Knit 4 rounds even.

Bind off all stitches very loosely.

Measure down Front and Back 8 (8½, 9, 9½)" from each shoulder seam; place a marker for armhole.

Using the tapestry needle and yarn, sew sleeves between markers; sew sleeve and side seams.

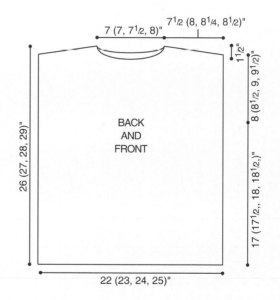

knit 10; join oasis ombre, knit 60; join a second strand of cream, knit 10. Work even as established for 14 rows total, ending after a wrong side row.

Next row: Knit 20 stitches as established (10 cream, 10 oasis ombre); join black, knit 40; join a second strand of oasis ombre, knit 10; using cream, knit 10. Work even as established for 14 rows total.

Next row: Knit 30 stitches as established (10 cream, 10 oasis ombre, 10 black); join another strand of oasis ombre, knit 20; join a second strand of black, knit 10; continue as established to end (10 oasis ombre, 10 cream). Work even as established for 16 rows total, cutting center oasis ombre strand after last row.

Next row: Knit 20 stitches as established (10 cream, 10 oasis ombre); using black, knit 40, cutting second strand of black as you come to it; continue as established to end (10 oasis ombre, 10 cream). Work even as established for 14 rows total, cutting black after last row.

Next row: Knit 10 cream; using oasis ombre, knit 60, cutting second strand of oasis ombre as you come to it; continue as established to end. Work even as established for 14 rows total, cutting oasis ombre after last row.

Next row: Using cream only, work even for 14 rows total.

Bind off all stitches.

## Finishing:

Weave in loose ends.

Fold piece in half, with right sides facing each other. Using the tapestry needle and black, sew side seams.

Sew lower edge together, beginning at each side seam and leaving a 9" opening at center for zipper.

Turn Pillow right side out; sew zipper into opening.

Pompoms (make 4): Cut several strands of black yarn, each 3 1/2" long. Hold strands together; using a longer strand of black, join strands tightly together at the center. Use the ends of the longer strand to attach one pompom to each corner of pillow.

Insert pillow form.

LEFT: *What do you make for Father's Day that he doesn't already have? His own pillow!*

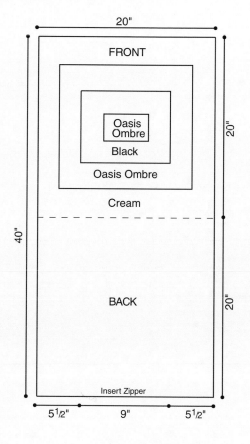

# suss resources

# suss shopping

Visit the Suss Design website (www.sussdesign.com) to purchase my line of yarns, knitting kits, knitwear, and other supplies and treats.

Visit my retail store for an even larger selection of these items and one-of-a-kind offerings.

SUSS DESIGN
7350 Beverly Boulevard
Los Angeles, CA 90036
(323) 954-9637
sales@sussdesign.com

Suss Knit Kits are available at most Barnes & Noble bookstores.

Suss Design knitwear is also available nationwide at NORDSTROM, SAKS FIFTH AVENUE, and ANTHROPOLOGIE, and at the following stores:

## CALIFORNIA

ANGEL
1221 Coast Village Road
Santa Barbara, CA 93108
(805) 565-1599

BILLY'S FASHION
18520 Burbank Boulevard
Tarzana, CA 91356
(818) 343-5332

BOULMICHE
9507 Santa Monica Boulevard
Beverly Hills, CA 90210
(310) 273-6443

LISA KLINE
136 S. Robertson Boulevard
Los Angeles, CA 90048
(310) 248-2423

PLANET BLUE
23410 Civic Center Way
Malibu, CA 90265
(310) 317-9975

ROUGE
9566 Dayton Way
Beverly Hills, CA 90210
(310) 273-1662

TRAFFIC
131 N. La Cienega Boulevard
Los Angeles, CA 90048
(310) 659-3438

## ILLINOIS

AMI AMI
720 Waukegan Road
Deerfield, IL 60015
(847) 940-0669

ETRE
1361 Northwells Street
Chicago, IL 60610
(312) 266-8101

MADISON & FRIENDS
940 N. Rush Street
Chicago, IL 60611
(312) 642-6403

TANGERINE
1659 N. Damen
Chicago, IL 60647
(773) 772-0505

## MASSACHUSETTS

VIA VAI
58 JFK Street
Cambridge, MA 02138
(617) 497-9959

## NEW YORK

INTERMIX
133 Fifth Avenue
New York, NY 10003
(212) 533-9720

SCOOP
532 Broadway
New York, NY 10012
(212) 431-1108

ZABARI
506 Broadway
New York, NY 10012
(212) 431-7502

**RHODE ISLAND**

GALAPAGOS
5193 Old Post Road
Charlestown, RI 02813
(401) 322-3000

**TEXAS**

KATIA
5638 Westheimer
Houston, TX 77056
(713) 621-1817

**VIRGINIA**

BLISS
1048 23rd Street
Roanoke, VA 24015
(540) 342-5995

# (KNIT AFFAIR RECIPES)

## valentine's day

### Elderberry Martini

**Serves 1**

*2 ounces elderberry juice (concentrated, available in specialty or natural food stores)*

*2 ounces Absolut vodka*

*1 ounce Triple sec*

*1 ounce club soda*

*Edible flowers, for garnish*

Shake all ingredients over ice and strain. Serve in a chilled martini glass. Garnish with edible flowers.

### Heart-Shaped Cakes with Smoked Salmon

This is a beautiful "finger food" that's perfect for Valentine's Day. Served with an elderberry martini—divine.

**Serves 6-8**

*3 large eggs*

*1/2 cup buttermilk*

*1/2 cup milk*

*1/2 cup vegetable oil, plus extra for cooking*

*1/2 teaspoon salt*

*1/2 teaspoon black pepper*

*1/2 cup spelt flour (or all-purpose flour)*

*1 teaspoon baking powder*

*Smoked salmon slices, cut into 2" pieces*

*1 6-ounce container crème fraîche (or sour cream)*

*Dill springs, for garnish*

In a large bowl, whisk together eggs and buttermilk until eggs are dissolved. Add milk, 1/2 cup oil, salt, and pepper. Add flour gradually, stirring until smooth. Add baking powder last, stirring until fully incorporated. Pour 1 tablespoon vegetable oil into a medium frying pan. When hot, pour batter into pan to cover bottom, approximately 1/2" thick. Fry until golden brown on bottom, then turn over and brown on other side. Remove to cutting board and cut into heart shapes using a 3-inch cookie cutter. Let cool. Garnish each cake with a thin slice of smoked salmon, a dab of crème fraîche, and a dill sprig.

## wedding shower brunch

### Bellinis

**Serves 6-8**

*1 bottle Champagne*

*Puree of 1 pound frozen or fresh peaches*

*Fresh raspberries, for garnish*

Fill champagne glasses with champagne, leaving about 1" of the glass empty at the top. Puree peaches and a little water in a blender (the water keeps the puree from getting too thick). Fill the champagne glasses with puree. Garnish with a fresh raspberry.

### Delicate Potato Cakes with Shrimp and Eggs (Potatiskakor med Räkoroch Ägg)

This dish is very popular in Sweden, served before dinner on a Saturday night with a glass of white wine.

**Serves 6-8**

*2 pounds peeled potatoes, grated (I prefer Yukon Gold potatoes)*

*1 teaspoon salt*

*1 teaspoon white pepper*

*4 tablespoons butter*

*6 hard-boiled eggs, thinly sliced*

*6 tablespoons mayonnaise*

*2 cups small bay shrimp, cooked and chilled*

*1 lemon, cut in half lengthwise and thinly sliced*

*Dill sprigs*

In a large bowl, season the grated potatoes with salt and pepper. Form potatoes into 3" pancakes and place on a flat plate. Melt the butter in a large skillet. Add the potato cakes and fry about 6 cakes at a time until crisp, about 10 to 15 minutes. Serve each cake immediately with 3 slices of hardboiled egg, 1 teaspoon mayonnaise, and 6 to 10 shrimp. Garnish with a lemon slice twisted around a small dill sprig.

### Buckwheat Cookies

I like to serve these cookies with fresh whipped cream and raspberries. The cookies are so rich in flavor, they make a perfect match.

MAKES ABOUT 2 DOZEN COOKIES

*1 cup buckwheat flour*

*2 tablespoons cocoa powder*

*1 1/2 teaspoons baking powder*

*1/2 teaspoon salt*

*1/2 stick (4 tablespoons) unsalted butter, at room temperature*

*1/2 cup vegetable oil*

*1/2 cup firmly packed dark brown sugar*

*1 cup granulated sugar*

*1 large egg*

*1 teaspoon vanilla*

*1 cup hazelnuts, finely chopped*

Preheat oven to 350° F. Line a baking sheet with foil or set aside a nonstick baking sheet. In a small mixing bowl, combine flour, cocoa powder, baking powder, and salt. Stir together until well blended and set aside. In a large mixing bowl, using a hand-held electric mixer set at medium speed, combine butter, oil, and brown and granulated sugars until smooth. Add egg and vanilla to the butter mixture and continue to beat until smooth. Gently stir in flour mixture, then add hazelnuts. Using a tablespoon, drop batter in mounds onto prepared pan, spacing the mounds about 1 1/2" apart. Bake for 12-14 minutes, until golden brown and dry to the touch when you dab your finger on top of a cookie.

# index

Paperback edition published in 2007 by Stewart, Tabori & Chang
An imprint of Harry N. Abrams, Inc.

Originally published in hardcover in 2004

Library of Congress Cataloging-in-Publication Data:

Cousins, Suss.
    Hollywood knits style : with 30 original suss designs/by Suss Cousins;
        Photography by Deborah Jaffe.
            p. cm.
ISBN-13: 978-1-58479-606-0
ISBN-10: 1-58479-606-5
    1. Knitting. 2. Knitting—Patterns.  I. Title.

TT820.C855 2004
746.43'2—dc22

                                    2004006105

Editor: Melanie Falick
Jacket design: Tanya Hughes
Interior design: Niloo Tehranchi
Production Manager: Jane Searle

The text of this book was composed in Interstate and Trade Gothic.

Printed and bound in China
10 9 8 7 6 5 4 3 2 1

**HNA** ▉▊▊▊
**harry n. abrams, inc.**
a subsidiary of La Martinière Groupe
115 West 18th Street
New York, NY 10011
www.hnabooks.com